Hazel's Homegrown

Dr Hazel Roberts

Bright Pen

Visit us online at www.authorsonline.co.uk

A Bright Pen Book

ISBN 0 7552 1015 8

Authors OnLine Ltd
40 Castle Street
Hertford SG14 1HR
England

This book is also available in e-book format, details of which are available at www.authorsonline.co.uk

CONTENTS

Introduction

You can grow food – whoever you are!

My first experience of growing vegetables was in the summer of 1997. I was renting a one-bedroom house in Milton Keynes with my partner, Steve. The garden was waist high in weeds and although the landlady had said she would sort it out, we volunteered to do it instead. That suited us as, unusually for a rented property, it meant we could do what we wanted with the garden. Steve had grown vegetables before and was keen to incorporate a small vegetable plot in this garden. So in the spring he dug over a 6 by 8-foot plot and we grew potatoes, broad beans, peas, mangetout, climbing beans and onions. As a complete novice, I was both surprised and delighted by how successful we were. It was a small plot and the ground was nothing more than clay with a good measure of builders' rubble thrown in, yet we had managed to grow food!

Our tenancy agreement came to an end whilst the climbing beans were still cropping frantically and we had to move house. We found another rented house nearby but this tenancy agreement unfortunately prohibited us from doing anything to the garden other than mow the lawn. However, the property did back onto allotments and we immediately applied for one.

By January 1998 we had our first allotment. It was considerably larger than our previous back garden plot and was equally overgrown with weeds. Steve spent 8 weeks double digging it before we were eventually able to get started. At this point we decided to invest £150 in our new hobby with which to buy all the tools and seeds we would need to get us started. I was curious to know whether we would get our initial investment back with the money we would save on vegetables. I made a note of the prices of vegetables from the supermarket and every time we harvested something, I weighed it and worked out its value. In the end, we had to spend another £50 on unbudgeted extras such as fertilisers, slug pellets and a second-hand freezer but the total value of produce from that first year came out as roughly £590.

I was totally surprised by how successful our first year was. Considering my inexperience and the fact that we both had full time jobs, I was amazed by what it was possible to grow with a bit of work every weekend. It seemed like a healthy pastime too, providing fresh air and exercise and such a prolific source of fresh produce that we ate far more fresh veg than we would otherwise have done.

In October 1998 we bought the house next door to the one we were renting so that we could be assured of a permanent place close to our allotment. In addition, we took over a second allotment plot and now work both of them between us, have a flourishing herb garden in our tiny front garden and several fruit trees in our small back garden. We manage to maintain them all with a little bit of work here and there at weekends and some evenings and are now self-sufficient in fruit and vegetables.

In the few years that I have been growing my own food I have learnt a great deal and have managed to become much more efficient. We are much better now at judging the quantities we need to grow to meet our demands, we are more aware of the danger signs to look out for and how to prevent losses, and we know what to do with the produce once it is grown. Perhaps most importantly, I have learnt what can and cannot be done to use and preserve the produce once it is harvested. This allows us to maximise the usefulness of what we grow.

We are just an ordinary couple, in an ordinary house, with full time jobs and children. We are neither Monty Don nor Delia Smith! I hope I have demonstrated by my own experience that growing your own food does not have to be expensive, time consuming or difficult and that it is possible to grow something, whatever your situation. It is a very rewarding pastime emotionally, physically and economically and hopefully this book will help you achieve success as easily as we did. This book is all based on my own experience. It is what I do, so I know it works!

How this book will help you

There is something uniquely special about serving up a delicious recipe made from your own grown fruit and vegetables. Firstly, you managed to grow plants from tiny seeds. Anyone who has ever done this will know how satisfying it can be. It seems almost like magic that plants can emerge from tiny specks of potential, but it is twice as rewarding when the plant you had a hand in creating then goes on to produce something you can eat. Then, with the right combination of ingredients and temperature, it is possible to turn those crops into delightful meals, desserts or accompaniments. And when all the hard work is forgotten and you sit down to eat, it really does feel as if you have got something for nothing.

The fact that you are reading this suggests that you have an interest in growing your own produce and eating it. There are, of course, other books on the market about growing vegetables, fruit and herbs, and there are other recipe books too. So how is this one different and why should it suit you?

I, of course, have a collection of books on gardening and on growing food. Although useful in their own ways, they do not serve my needs as I would like. Firstly, they generally arrange the vegetables in alphabetical order and have a page or two dedicated to each. This can be very useful when I am interested in that particular crop but it is not how I work most of the time. Instead, I work with time. In April, for example, I want to know what I should be doing with all of my crops. What needs to be planted, what crops will I have and are there any danger signs I should look out for? I want to make sure I don't forget anything that I should be doing. Apart from reading about every vegetable and looking for the word April, I would not be able to get this information from conventional gardening books. In this book, however, everything is arranged month by month. I guess this does make it harder to look up something for a particular crop but chances are you won't need to because you will already have read what you wanted to know at the time that you needed to know it.

Growing fruit and vegetables will quickly become an ongoing hobby. There should always be something that needs doing and always something to harvest too. Clearly, however, it will take at least a couple of months from starting before you have your first crop. The first year, therefore, is slightly different from subsequent years and I have tried to cater for this by providing information on "first year" and "subsequent years" so that this book is useful whether you have never grown food before or whether you are well established. I have started this book in January but it is possible start using it in any month. However, you may find it beneficial to read some of the planning and organisational tips given in the January chapter whatever month you start in.

Another disadvantage of other vegetable books is that they tend to be rather too thorough with their descriptions of the pests and diseases likely to affect a particular crop. Sure, that kind of information is handy if your crops have come down with something horrible and you would like to identify it. However, I feel that reading a whole page on what can go wrong before you have even started can be very demoralising. Anyone would think that growing vegetables was difficult and liable to failure. You may well find the odd crop here and there that you just

3

can't get to grow successfully but, on the whole, growing fruit and vegetables is very straightforward. In my experience each crop seems to have one or two pests or problems that are likely to affect it and in most cases they can be either prevented or ignored. So I mention at the relevant time what danger signs to look out for and what preventative methods are required. I feel this is much more useful than a diagnosis of what has gone wrong from a whole list of horrors that are unlikely to happen.

In my opinion, the most significant downfall of most fruit and vegetable books is a lack of information on what to do with the food once you have grown it. Firstly, they often don't tell you how much to grow in the first place, so you end up with a huge glut and then no clue how to deal with it. Unfortunately, home-grown produce does not come with handy labels that tell you how to prepare, cook or preserve it and that is not the sort of information provided on seed packs or in gardening books either. So perhaps the answer would be to buy another book or two on preserving or cooking with vegetables. Unfortunately, these do not provide the solution either. The major drawback of these books is that they are geared towards people of the modern society who can buy any fruit or vegetable from the supermarket at any time of year, regardless of whether it is in season or not. It is quite surprising the numbers of recipes to be found with ingredients that are just not ready at the same time. Even classic combinations such as apple and blackcurrant ripen at different times of the year. In addition, you will not find a book that deals with everything from freezing to pickling to eating it fresh. Furthermore, preserving books rarely tell you what to do with the preserves once you have made them!

In this book I have attempted to provide guidelines on the numbers of plants you should aim to grow in the first place, as this is probably the best way to avoid gluts. Variety is the key here. Grow small amounts of a lot of different crops. Not only does this stop you becoming bored by day after day of the same crop, but plants are ready at different times so this method gives you crops over a longer period. If you get it right, you can have fresh crops all year round.

However, you will, either intentionally or accidentally, have gluts of certain foods. A glut of some things is desirable simply so that you can preserve it and enjoy it out of season. I have therefore tried to include suggestions on how to preserve your produce and have indicated where a preserving method, such as freezing, just doesn't work for that crop. But, as I have already implied, preserving it is not the end of the story. It is essential to know what to do with the preserved food once you have made it. There is absolutely no point in producing jars and jars of something if you either don't know when to use it or don't like the stuff. It will just end up taking up storage space until you eventually decide it is too old and throw it away. So a good tip here is, firstly, don't grow a crop if you don't like it, and secondly, don't make a preserve unless you know what you are going to do with it (even if it is just to give it away at Christmas!). I have provided suggestions for what to do with each recipe I have included. Check these out before you go ahead to make sure you will like and use it.

Whether you get a glut or not, you will, of course, be wanting to eat as much fresh produce as possible. There is nothing quite like eating freshly picked fruit and vegetables that are just bursting with vitamins. Once you have done that you will wonder exactly how old supermarket veg is when you buy it and will be surprised by how much flavour things have. For example, I never realised that carrots have a flavour until I grew some! So having put all that effort in, the last thing you want to do now is turn it into a tasteless mush by cooking it badly. That is why I have also provided suggested preparation and cooking guidelines for each crop.

You should now see that this book is designed with you in mind. It is arranged in time order for your convenience so you know what you should be doing and what you should be looking for throughout the year. I have tried to keep the growing side of things as simple as possible because it is easy as long as you do a little bit often. Then once you have successfully grown your own food I have provided ideas and information on what to do with it. With any luck you will then have fresh produce and a store cupboard bursting with homemade treats that will keep you supplied all year. Together with a warm feeling of satisfaction.

How to use this book

Firstly, don't be put off by the quantity of information in this book. You don't have to grow everything I have mentioned or make every recipe. This information is for a wide audience, so pick and choose what you want from it. If you successfully grow potatoes, onions and carrots in your first year, enjoy it, and be pleased with your achievement.

Each monthly chapter is divided up according to experience. If you are just starting out, you will need to refer to the "First year" section of each chapter. This gives guidance on things, such as planning a plot, that only need to be done once. Later in the year you will also have to refer to the "Every year" section that deals with annual tasks that always need to be done no matter how experienced you are. By the end of the year you will have worked through the book once and will be ready to start the next season. Hopefully all the one-off jobs will have been completed and you will have other things to do because your plot has developed. You now need to refer to the "Subsequent years" section, and will need to refer to the "Every year" and "Subsequent years" sections for as long as you continue to grow produce. If you grow something new then look back in the "first year" section for information on how to get started with that crop.

Each of these sections is divided into subsections that deal with both the gardening and the cookery. The sections "Things to do" and "Things to expect" explain what needs doing on the plot and what positive signs and problems to look out for. The sections "Things to harvest" and "Harvesting tips" explain what you can potentially expect to be ready to eat and how to get it into the kitchen. The next sections deal with the produce once it has reached the kitchen. These include the "Cooking tips" and "Preserving tips" that explain how to use the produce fresh or how to freeze, pickle, dry or store the produce until needed. The "In the Kitchen" section provides a selection of recipes that use that month's seasonal produce (and/or produce from storage) and includes preserving recipes such as jams or chutney as well as ideas for using the fresh produce in meals.

January

January is the time to first start thinking about the kitchen garden. It is the time to plan, sort and organise yourself ready for the growing season ahead.

The weather in January can be problematic and off putting but there are jobs that need to be done inside. These are the designing and planning jobs that are best done in a warm armchair with a cup of tea and optimistic thoughts of the months ahead.

First Year

Things to do

Planning your kitchen garden

Although this is in the January chapter, this information is useful no matter what time of year you start your kitchen garden. It is, however, ideal to start during the dormant months between October and February, as it is easiest to get the weeds under control during these cold months and helps you get the plot ready in time for the beginning of the growing season in March.

Size

The first thing to do is to plan the area you will be using to grow vegetables. The size of the vegetable garden will be constrained to some extent by the maximum space available to you. However, you need to think about how ambitious you intend to be. It can be a mistake to attempt too much in the first season, then struggle, fail and be put off altogether. This is particularly true if the area you are going to use is currently rough ground. No matter how carefully you prepare the ground, weeds will come back and haunt you and if you take on too much you may become demoralised. It might be better, therefore, to just tackle a small area to begin with and gradually cultivate the rest of the land over the subsequent years. You also need to think about the crops that you intend to grow, as the plants vary greatly in size. However, you can achieve amazing results in a surprisingly small amount of soil (or even clay and builders' rubble!) so don't be put off by thinking you don't have the space. Below are some suggestions on how you might structure your vegetable garden and this will help you decide how much space you need.

Location

The site you choose for the vegetables will probably be dictated to you. If you have an allotment then the location has been determined for you. If you have a garden there may only be one place for your vegetable garden to go. In general, however, vegetables need good sunlight and to be fairly sheltered from prevailing winds. It may, therefore, be necessary to remove over-shading or to put in some sort of wind screening. You may also need to think about some sort of fencing if hungry rabbits, badgers (they love sweetcorn), or deer might trouble you.

Raised Bed System

Having preliminarily decided on the site and size of your kitchen garden you now need to decide how it will look and how you will plant it. It is generally accepted these days that a raised bed system is beneficial over the conventional allotment type row planting. In the raised bed system, beds are set up for planting and pathways run between them. This has several advantages. Firstly, you should never have to walk on the soil, which can damage the soil structure and can limit the times of the year that you can access the beds. Secondly, it can lead to easier management of crop rotation to prevent the depletion of nutrients and the accumulation of diseases. It also reduces the amount of digging that is required.

If using the raised bed system you need to decide what size each bed will be. It should ideally be no wider than 5 feet (1.5 metres) so that it is possible to access the middle of the bed from the paths without having to tread on the soil. The length of the bed is less of an issue and will probably be determined by the space available, the way it looks and a compromise between good access and loss of growing space to paths. If the beds are very long, however, you might be tempted to walk across the soil rather than walk round!

It is more aesthetically pleasing to edge the beds with something. The edging can be made from any number of different materials, the choice of which will come down to personal preference, what is available and finances. Edging can be made from material such as brick, wood or plastic. It is best, however, to avoid tannalised wood as there is some evidence to suggest that chemicals, such as arsenic, can leach out of the wood into your soil and could potentially end up in your crops. It is simplest and cheapest to have raised beds that are not edged, with the soil simply mounded up rising slightly to the middle of the bed. Soil may from time to time escape onto the paths but can be easily scooped back onto the beds. This has the advantage of not having the problem of weeds growing so close to the edging that they are difficult to deal with or the problems of slugs and snails nestling in the shelter that the edging provides.

Paths
The paths between the beds are also an important consideration. Again, looks and finances will be the main consideration. There is little point taking up valuable growing space with wide paths but the paths should be wide enough to allow access with a wheelbarrow. For this reason a minimum width of about 20 inches (50 cm) is recommended. Some people have grass paths between their beds. These are successful if it is possible to gain easy access to keep them well mown, otherwise they will become laden with weeds and will spread into the beds. If your vegetable garden is on a remote site such as an allotment then don't forget there is unlikely to be an electricity supply to plug in electric mowers and strimmers. Hard surface paths are probably better because they can be walked on during wet weather but they can be more expensive. If finances allow and you are confident the site will be permanent then it is probably worthwhile investing in a decent hard surface path such as gravel or paving. If on the other hand finances are more of an issue than the way it looks then old carpet or boards might be a better alternative. Just make sure the surface will not be slippery when wet and muddy.

Square Foot Gardening
The raised bed system can be taken to the extreme known as square foot gardening. This is an idea that came over from America in the mid-eighties but can be very useful for those just starting out. In this system a raised bed of 4 feet (120 cm) by 4 feet is made and then the bed is divided up using string or other similar markers into 16 one square foot (30 cm) plots. A different crop is then planted in each square foot. This system can be useful if you have a very limited space or if you are just starting and want to start small. It can also be a great way of introducing children to vegetable growing by giving them their very own mini vegetable garden. Because such a small area is employed, maintenance is easy and cropping is intensive. If this sounds like a good idea but just a bit small for your ambitions then maybe consider having several 4 feet plots. In this case you could have one or two plots divided into 16 squares for your smaller crops and then others given over solely for larger crops such as potatoes, courgettes and pumpkins.

Pots and Containers

If space is particularly limited then it is possible to grow a surprisingly large selection of fruit, vegetables and herbs in pots. This has the added advantage of being portable; something to consider if you are living in a rented property. One of my first experiences of vegetable growing was in a rented house where we were prohibited from doing anything to the garden other than maintaining it. We still managed to have a flourishing herb garden in the window box, potatoes in the dustbin and peppers, cucumbers and tomatoes in grow-bags in the back garden.

Herbs are excellent plants for containers and can be grown inside in pots or outside in window boxes, hanging baskets, grow-pouches, or tubs. Herbs provide all year greenery and some very attractive flowers as well as having culinary and medicinal uses. Because many herbs come from Mediterranean regions they are relatively drought tolerant, which is ideal for containers, as they tend to dry out easily. Some herbs, such as mint, can be invasive if allowed to grow directly in the soil so it is best to restrict it to pots even if the pot is then sunk into the ground. Trailing herbs are particularly pleasing in hanging baskets and window boxes. Herbs are most useful if they are close to the kitchen so that you can nip out and grab a spring of rosemary for dinner with ease. Pots may be the best option to get the herbs close to where they are needed.

Tomatoes, peppers and cucumbers all grow well in grow-bags or pots and can be grown inside or out if the right varieties are selected and there is enough light. Trailing cherry tomatoes are also an attractive option for a hanging basket.

Some potatoes can be grown in purpose-made potato bins. In this case some compost is put in the bottom of the bin, then 5 or 6 tubers are added before being covered with more compost. As the plants grow, you simply add more compost rather than "earthing up" the potatoes. When it comes to harvesting them the bottom of the tub is opened and the potatoes can be pulled out. Of course, this is just as affective and considerably cheaper if an old dustbin is used. Just remember to put some drainage holes in it. To harvest, simply tip the whole bin up and empty it. It is worth knowing, however, that early potato varieties, best for new potatoes, only produce new tubers from above the seed potato. It is therefore essential that compost be added above as the plants grow, as you cannot plant it shallowly and expect potatoes to form lower down. Maincrop potatoes do produce new tubers both above and below the seed potato but they are less suitable for growing in pots because they need more room.

Strawberries are another edible crop that is often grown in pots. Purpose-made strawberry pots are available but any suitable container can be used. They can also be grown in grow-pouches and hanging baskets. Other fruit for containers are dwarf fruit trees such as mini peach, apple or pear trees. These grow no taller than 3 feet (1 metre) but can have a surprisingly high yield for their size. Gooseberries and currants pruned into half standards are another attractive possibility for tubs. In fact, more and more fruit varieties suitable for container growing are appearing on the market so it is worth checking out the catalogues.

There are also dwarf bean varieties that can be grown attractively in patio pots. You might like to try a few peas or even some short rooted carrot varieties.

Potager
Yet another way to grow edible crops is to incorporate them into an ornamental garden. This method is known as the potager. There are some obvious advantages to this method, particularly its attractive appearance. Most vegetable plants are attractive in their own right. Take the delicate feathery foliage of carrots or the purple foliage of beetroot or red cabbage for example. There are also attractive flowers or fruits such as runner beans or peppers. Carefully selecting the varieties can enhance this – use a purple flowering and purple podded bean for example. Another advantage is that the vegetables can be planted with "companion" flowering plants. Companion plants have some sort of beneficial affect on the fruit or vegetable they are planted with, such as attracting beneficial insects, deterring pests or enhancing growth.

There are, of course, disadvantages with the potager. Firstly, there is less space available for vegetables so yields will be lower than in the same space dedicated solely to vegetables. Crop rotation can be difficult to organise and track. The need or desire to keep it attractive can mean a higher financial demand, particularly for the hard landscaping aspects. And how do you solve the problem of a patch of ugly bare ground when you have harvested your crop?

Recommendation
When deciding which method of vegetable gardening you will employ you have to think carefully about what will best suit you, the plot you

have and the outcome you have in mind. However, I would recommend that you use ideas from each of these methods. For example, on my allotment I use the raised bed method. I am striving for high yields, easy management and utilitarian, cheap hard landscaping. However, I also have several four feet plots for the kids, which they use with success and enthusiasm. And even on the allotment there is room for attractive flowering plants as companions to the vegetables. I grow my herbs mostly in the sunny front garden. Here they are arranged as an attractive rockery and are grown for their appearance as much as their use. In addition, they are close to home so they are easy to use, even in the middle of winter. Tender herbs are grown inside on the windowsill. In the back garden I have mini fruit trees in pots.

Having decided on the size, site and style of your kitchen garden it is worthwhile making a plan on paper. Take some measurements on the area and draw a scale diagram of the plot with its beds or planting locations. Then you can start planning what to grow.

Dealing with rubbish
When planning your kitchen garden don't forget that you will generate rubbish of various sorts. It is worthwhile incorporating ways of dealing with this into your plan. There are four types of rubbish that you will generate.

The first, and most important, is organic waste that can be composted so allow space for a compost bin of some sort in your plan. This can be of any of numerous designs, hand made or purpose built. You can compost garden waste and kitchen scraps.   This includes grass cuttings, fallen leaves, vegetable peelings, egg shells, tea bags and leftover or stale vegetables. Ideally the pieces should be small and you should avoid thick layers of one type of waste (e.g. when adding grass cuttings, mix it up with other waste). It should not include any woody material that will not compost readily or diseased plant material, as this could transfer the disease to your compost and subsequently to the soil. You should also avoid adding meat to your compost as this can attract vermin, such as rats.

Secondly, you will have inorganic, completely useless rubbish that needs to be thrown away, or recycled if the facilities are available. This will be mostly plastic – bags and containers. Diseased plants and woody material that won't compost need to be either thrown in the bin or burnt. You may also generate organic waste that is too coarse to compost quickly but that will decay in time. If you can afford a shredder then that may be the solution or, alternatively you need another compost bin that you can leave for considerably longer and that will produce lower grade compost.

To be organic or not?
There is increasing concern over the possible contamination of food with chemicals and more and more people are choosing to buy so called organic food, and supermarkets are ever increasing their ranges to keep up with this. Growing your own food is an ideal way to keep control over the chemicals that you eat. However, you may want to consider having a bit more flexibility over being "organic" than a commercial grower wishing to use that term would have. I think it is important to keep a sense of realism and to not enter into organic gardening with zealous fanaticism. I have seen several people take on adjacent allotment plots with buckets of enthusiasm and a determination to grow their produce totally organically. However, a few months later, they give up on the whole thing in part due to crops failing before they have started because of the dreaded slug. Just a degree of flexibility and some common sense can mean your produce is good and wholesome and a hundred times better than conventional supermarket vegetables whilst not technically being "organic".

If you produce your own compost or have a source of manure available to you then you can supply all or most of your fertiliser needs organically. You can also buy organic fertilisers, such as chicken manure and blood, fish and bone. However, artificial fertilisers such as growmore or tomato feed can be more convenient sometimes and supply the nutrients to the plants in a more accessible form that the plants can take in more quickly. Both provide exactly the same essential nutrients in the end. Of course, compost and manure also improve soil structure in a way that growmore doesn't and I believe both have their place.

Increasingly more and more chemical pesticides are being withdrawn from market. This rings alarm bells with me and a pest has to be particularly rampant before I consider using a chemical spray insecticide. Another concern is that some kill all insects, including the beneficial ones such as hoverflies, ladybirds and bees, although they should carry a special warning if this is the case. Usually periodic squashing of pests can keep them under control. Failing that, soapy water or a strong hose can blast them off the plants and slow them down. I also tolerate numerous pests because they don't do serious harm. I have, however, resorted to using a copper fungicide to save a crop from mildew or blight. This is a traditional method and does not harm insects.

Controlling slugs and snails is a surprisingly controversial subject. There are a number of suggested methods for dispatching them, from beer traps to salty water to slug pellets. I would have to have so many beer traps on my allotment that it would simply not be viable. Equally, I don't have the time or the patience for after dark hunting of slugs and snails and dropping them into salt water. Anyone who tells you that slugs and snails will not walk across rough surfaces such as grit or broken eggs shells clearly hasn't seen them doing it! So, I do unfortunately resort to slug pellets for certain crops at particular times of the year as the only alternative to losing the crop. Once poisoned, the slug becomes so unattractive that I really don't believe any bird or hedgehog would consider eating one. However, if this is a concern, then it is possible to place the pellets under cover where slugs can reach them but other animals can't, or to net the area to prevent birds eating the slugs. Some people choose to place slug pellets as if they were nuggets of gold, rather than sprinkling them indiscriminately and this seems to have success too. The decision is down to you and with experience you will decide what works best for you within your principles.

I would not really recommend the use of chemical weedkillers. Some can be quite persistent in the soil and it can be difficult to avoid "overspray". Some plants, such as brassicas are particularly sensitive to even the merest hint of weedkiller and will be affected by overspray. Be particularly aware of this if you are on a communal plot such as allotments. Physically digging up and removing the weeds is the best method and the most precise, although it can also be very hard work. If you have a large area that needs all the weeds removing then cover it up with black plastic or old carpet (preferably not foam-backed) and come back to it in a year's time. For small areas, try a "weedwand" or flame gun that will destroy the weed by heat. Around crops, use a hoe or pull them up by hand. The key really is to keep on top of the weeds so that it is never a big job, although in reality this is often difficult to achieve.

Deciding what to grow
Deciding what to grow can be enormous fun or a complete nightmare, depending on whether you enjoy making decisions from a huge range of options. I would recommend growing most vegetables from seeds and buying most fruit as plants. One way to do this would be to go to your nearest garden centre (or even your supermarket!) and have a

look at what seeds they have or what plants are available. Alternatively, you could get yourself a selection of seed catalogues and do all your shopping from the comfort of an armchair. There are several advantages to this, not least the comfort factor! Firstly, many seed catalogues will give you offers with each order such as discounts or free seeds, which you may not get from garden centres. Secondly, you can compare one catalogue with another and find exactly the variety you want for the best price. I find that each year I will spread my seed order over several catalogues to get the best deal. Another advantage is that although seed orders tend to be dispatched immediately, orders of onion sets, seed potatoes, or plants should be dispatched only when the time is right to plant them out. I would then only use garden centres later on if I underestimated the number of seeds I needed.

Estimating the number of seeds you will need in the first season can be difficult. Remember, though, that most seeds remain viable for several years (longer than it usually says on the packet) so it does not matter if you get too many. Just store them in a cool, dry place until next year. This is not true for things like seed potatoes and onion sets, however, which must be planted that year.

When choosing varieties look at the planting out and harvest times. Try to get a succession of vegetables throughout the summer at least, if not throughout the year. So, for example, order several varieties of peas that crop at different times. Go for varieties that appeal to you – are they "reliable", "easy to grow" or slightly out of the ordinary. It is great fun to grow varieties of familiar vegetables that you cannot buy in the supermarket – like round carrots, golden beetroot or round cucumbers. I strongly recommend going for variety, though. Select 2 or 3 types of most crops and only sow a few of each. You are then much more likely to find a variety that does well on your plot, one with appealing looks or taste and it is much more interesting to grow and eat a selection of things. Just don't be tempted to sow the whole lot – store the surplus seeds until next year. With potato and onion varieties, choose small bags of each to get your variety – it may work out a bit more expensive but it is worth it.

Choosing Seeds
Every year you will need to decide what you want to grow and then buy the appropriate seeds for your annual vegetables. Below are some guidelines of what sort of things you might consider for each crop. I have deliberately not mentioned specific varieties as there are many varieties out there and I would not want to influence your choice

because what is suitable for me might not be for you and anyway trying different things is part of the fun. Besides, new seed varieties are always coming out and this section would need constantly updating if varieties were mentioned. The considerations below refer to seeds you need to grow from spring to summer. Information on autumn varieties can be found in the July chapter and information on herbs can be found in the March chapter. Vegetables that are not grown from seed (such as potatoes) are dealt with in the next section below. It is possible to plant fruit trees, bushes and canes, anytime between November and February whilst the plants are dormant. However, it is possibly better to start this in November before the soil cools down rather than hope for a warm day in the new year when the ground isn't frozen. It is essential to prepare the ground well for fruit planting and this takes time. As you will probably have plenty to keep you busy with site preparation and vegetable growing to start with, it is probably advisable to leave fruit planting until November. For this reason I have included the advice about fruit varieties in the November chapter but if you wish to get started with fruit now, simply read the relevant section in that chapter.

Aubergines
If you intend to grow aubergines outside then you must choose an outdoor variety. The main differences between aubergine varieties are the size and colour of the fruit. Of course, conventional aubergines have large, black fruit but you might consider red or white fruiting varieties or even mini varieties. The mini fruit varieties are particularly useful if you are growing them in a container or if you are growing them outside, as they are ready sooner and more like to be available before the frost. They also have advantages in the kitchen if you only use a small amount of aubergine at any one time.

Beetroots
You will probably find one variety of beetroot that grows well and you particularly like, so you grow it year after year. A bolt resistant, dark red, round variety is always good but you might consider other, more novel, varieties such as elongated shaped roots or yellow, pink or white varieties. Certainly a combination of different coloured varieties looks good when served up as part of a salad or buffet. Pale varieties taste the same but don't stain, so can be useful in that respect.

Broad beans
It is possible to sow some broad beans in both autumn and spring, but at this time of year any variety can be sown. Variations between varieties include differences in flower colour, bean colour and pod size.

The most common flower colour is white and black but all white and all crimson flowered varieties are also available and are very attractive. Seed colour variations are subtler and are various shades of green. Pods vary from short ones with a few beans to longer pods with more beans. There are also subtle differences in flavour, with some being distinctly "beanier" than others.

Broccoli
Broccoli can be divided into calabrese and sprouting broccoli types. Calabrese produces one large, central head initially, followed by smaller florets, is ready to eat in the summer and is what is usually labelled as broccoli in shops. Sprouting broccoli only produces smaller florets and is generally ready in March to April, although some varieties can be ready as early as December in a good year. It is a very useful early crop and comes in purple and white varieties. There is little difference between varieties, except some have more compact plants and some have more tender stems that can also be eaten.

Cabbage
Cabbage is one of those vegetables I dislike so tend not to grow. However, I have always like pickled red cabbage so I do grow this. There are different types of cabbage that can be harvested at different times of the year so it is possible to eat cabbage, should you wish to, all year round. However, as there are so many other things to eat during the summer, I feel that cabbage is of most use during the winter when other crops are scarce. This is one reason why I grow red cabbage, as it can be harvested from autumn and stands well over winter. It can be pickled, added to stir-fries, cooked with spices at Christmas, or just plain boiled, making it, in my opinion, more versatile than green cabbage.

Carrots
Although carrot varieties are much of a muchness, there are a few things to consider when choosing seeds. Firstly, if you have a problem with carrot root fly (which is very likely) then a resistant variety will be of use. If your soil is compacted, shallow or stony (even after cultivation) then a short rooted variety is more likely to be successful. Personally, I prefer short root or medium root types because they are easier to pull out of the ground than long tapering ones. If you have sandy soil or want to win prizes with your carrots then tapering varieties are for you. A novelty that is particularly popular with children is round carrots. This can also be grown in containers because of its shallow root.

Celery

Unless you want the hassle of growing celery in trenches, I would recommend a self-blanching type. You may also consider a more novel colour, such as golden or pink. If you mainly use celery as a flavouring in dishes such as soup or casserole, then a leaf celery would also be suitable, although a seed stockist is harder to find.

Courgettes

The variations in courgette are mainly in colour and shape. The most conventional types are long, green ones but yellow ones and round ones are available. Round courgettes can either be eaten when ping-pong ball size or allowed to grow larger and stuffed.

Cucumbers

If you don't have a greenhouse it is essential that you select an outdoor variety of cucumber. It is best to grow an all-female variety or else your cucumbers might be bitter. "Burpless" varieties are also worth considering if you suffer in that way. On the novelty side, round or yellow varieties are available but by the time they are sliced and on your plate you can't tell that they were ever round.

French beans

The two main types of French bean are dwarf and climbing varieties. Dwarf types grow no more than 2 feet tall and do not require staking. They are more convenient if you do not wish to use stakes and they can be grown in pots. They tend to crop sooner than climbing beans too. However, they take up the same amount of ground space as the same number of climbing bean plants and give a considerably lower yield. Narrow, cylindrical podded beans and broad, flat podded beans are both available. The cylindrical bean makes very elegant looking fine beans when young but, by weight, give an overall lower yield generally than the flat podded beans. However, I have always found French beans to crop abundantly and, if anything, a lower yield is something of a blessing. It is also possible to grow varieties with yellow pods or purple foliage, flowers and/or pods. These are particularly attractive whilst growing, although the purple coloration is lost on cooking.

Gherkins

There is little or no choice in gherkin varieties.

Kale

The main consideration here is whether you want flat leaf kale or curly kale. Personally, I grow curly leaf because it is more attractive. Then you need to decide whether you want green or purple leaves. The green leaf varieties tend to crop slightly better than the purple but the purple makes a very attractive plant. When cooked the purple kale becomes dark green.

Lablab beans
These are climbing beans with attractive pink flowers and unusual shaped, purple podded beans. They make an unusual bean on the plate and an attractive addition to the plot.

Leeks
Different leek varieties have subtly different foliage colours, ranging from pale green to an almost blue green. There are also differences in potential size, with some large varieties available. However, the eventual size produced is much more dependent on growing position and length of time they are in the ground.

Lettuce
There are probably hundreds of lettuce varieties and you probably already know the type you like to use. It is also one of the more common types of seeds to be given away free on gardening magazines or with seed orders so you may end up with several varieties without even trying. However, one thing you might like to consider is whether the lettuce "hearts up" or is loose leaf. If it forms a heart then you have to harvest a whole lettuce at a time. If it is loose leaf then you can remove individual leaves as and when required. As lettuce doesn't store well for long periods, if you only eat a small amount of lettuce at a time then you should probably grow a loose leaf variety or a small cos type. You may also consider a red or curly leaf type to add visual interest.

Mangetout
Mangetout can be subdivided into two types – those that are eaten when the pods are flat and the peas undeveloped and sugar pea types where the peas are fully developed and they are eaten pod and all. The flat type is ready first, is high yielding and one of the first new season crops. The sugar peas follow on later when peas are also ready.

Melons
Most melon varieties are only suitable for growing in a greenhouse so check carefully that the variety is suitable for outdoor growth if you do not have a greenhouse. Outdoor varieties are rarer so you will have less choice of melon type. It is best, where you can, to choose to grow

the type of melon you like to eat so read the description in the catalogue or on the packet carefully. A word of caution – growing melons, particularly outside, is not easy and probably best avoided for a few seasons until you are more confident.

Parsnips

Parsnips are notoriously difficult to get to germinate. Once you have found a reliable variety, stick with it.

Peas

There are two main types of peas – wrinkled and smooth peas. In general, smooth peas are planted later than wrinkled. A succession in peas can be achieved either by sowing more than one variety with different maturing times, or by sowing one variety at two-week intervals. Later pea varieties often suffer from lack of water and do not crop as well as earlier ones. Modern pea varieties tend to grow to 2 to 3 feet tall and have white flowers and green pods. However, heritage varieties can have novel features, such as 4 to 6 feet height and purple flowers and pods. Another variation worth considering is a petit pois type, which grows pods stuffed full of small peas. You may also come across asparagus peas. These are a type of vetch with a sprawling habit, crimson flowers and unusual winged seedpods. They are so called because they are supposed to taste like asparagus although I'm not convinced. It is essential that they be picked when very young because they quickly become tough and inedible but as they are an abundant cropper, it is difficult to pick them often enough. However, the attractive crimson flower makes a pretty addition to the plot.

Peppers

There are numerous pepper varieties to choose from, although most are only suitable for growing in a greenhouse. There are two main types of pepper – sweet (capsicum) and chilli peppers. Both types are difficult to grow outside but can be done successfully in a good season. Capsicum varieties mainly differ in the size and colour of the fruit, whereas chilli peppers also vary in strength of flavour. However, only more mild flavoured chilli's can be grown outside. Compact plants with small fruit are suitable for growing in containers and most varieties are suitable for grow bags.

Pumpkins

Choose the variety of pumpkin based on its intended use. If it is for a Halloween lantern then choose an attractive orange, spherical type. If it is for culinary uses then smaller pumpkins are more practical. If, on the other hand, your ambition is to grow the world's largest pumpkin then a large variety will be required!

Spring onions
There is little difference between varieties, although red spring onions make an attractive addition to salads. It is worth, however, having both spring and winter hardy types for an all year round crop (see also July).

Sweetcorn
When choosing a sweetcorn variety to grow you may come across the term "supersweet". These varieties were devised for supermarkets, where the corns are left for quite some time before they are eventually eaten. The sweetness of sweetcorn starts to decline from the moment it is picked so the extra sweetness of "supersweets" allows for some deterioration to occur but there to still be a sweet flavour when eaten. As you will undoubtedly eat your corn sooner from a homegrown plant, supersweet varieties are not essential but they can be grown if you wish. In addition to conventional yellow types, you can get bicolour and multicolour sweetcorn varieties. The bicolours are yellow and white and the multicolours are yellow, red and blue (yes, really!). Multicolours tend to take longer to mature and by the time the colour is really strong the cobs have passed their best and are a bit tough. However, they are a nice novelty and might be something you consider if you have space. If you are intending to grow more than one variety that are significantly different to each other (e.g. supersweet/normal or yellow/bicolour), you will need to space the two varieties far enough apart to avoid cross-pollination. If this happens then the characteristics can become merged. It is also worth considering varieties that mature at different times. F1 hybrid types produce cobs that are all ripe at the some time so the only way to extend the harvest season is to choose more than one variety with different maturing times. This helps to prevent cross-pollination too, as the pollen is ripe at different times. You may also like to try growing mini sweetcorn that you eat whole, although the plants take up the same amount of space. It is, however, difficult to judge when the cobs are big enough, but still tender enough, to eat. They quickly become over mature, tough and inedible.

Tomatoes
There are literally hundreds of tomato varieties but there are some things you might like to consider when choosing a variety. Firstly, if you don't have a greenhouse, it is essential you choose an outdoor variety. Next, you need to decide what size fruit you want – cocktail,

cherry, plum, beefsteak etc. Then there is the colour of the fruit desired – red, yellow, green, white, purple, pink, brown, stripy etc. Finally, you need to decide whether you want cordon or bush-type plants. Cordons are grown as a single stem up a support, removing side-shoots as they grow. They require the most amount of maintenance but produce the highest yields. Bush type can be allowed to do their own thing but the yields are generally lower. Bush types are suitable for growing in pots and both types can be grown in grow bags.

Watercress

Recently it has become more widely accepted that it is possible to grow watercress without access to running water. Previously land cress has been grown as an acceptable substitute as it can be grown in normal conditions. In order to grow watercress you will need poorly drained soil. If this is not available naturally then growing it in a container with few or no drainage holes can achieve this.

Non-seed vegetables

Asparagus

Although asparagus can be grown from seed it is more successful if grown from crowns. If grown from seed it will be 3 years before the plants are big enough to withstand a harvest. However, if you buy 1-year-old crowns, you will be able to harvest asparagus from the next year after planting. All male crowns are better as the plants don't waste energy producing seeds and they do not self-seed in unwanted areas.

Garlic

Garlic is best grown from bulbs divided into cloves. There is little to choose between varieties but it is best to grow varieties sold specifically for growing in this country rather than using bulbs you bought for eating. Many of the shop sold varieties for eating are imported and only grow well in Mediterranean conditions. You may also consider growing elephant garlic, which, although huge, has a mild flavour.

Onions

Although it is possible to grow onions from seeds, it is more reliable to grow onions from sets (mini-onions ready for planting) and this method produces a more uniform bulb size. The main difference between varieties grown at this time of year is the colour of the skin. The most conventional type has brown skin but white and red skinned varieties are available and have their own distinct flavours. Heat-treated onion sets are preferred, as they are less prone to bolting and can be planted later.

Potatoes

There are numerous potato varieties and numerous reasons for choosing a particular variety. If you have space, it is worth growing more than one type to increase the availability throughout the year and the culinary uses.

The first way that potatoes are categorised is into 3 groups relating to harvesting times – first early, second early and main crop. First early potatoes are ready as new potatoes around July, tend to give a lower yield but suffer less from problems such as slug damage and blight than main crops, which are ready from August.

Next, potatoes can be distinguished by their culinary uses and texture into waxy and floury types. Waxy potatoes boil well and make excellent new or salad potatoes. Floury types are better chipped, roasted or baked and some can disintegrate readily after only a short amount of boiling.

Other differences include the colour of the skin and flesh and resistance to problems such as eelworm, scab and blight.

You may already have a favourite potato variety based on what you like to eat but with a few years of experimentation you will find one or several varieties that suit both your growing conditions and your culinary tastes. Each year we try to grow about 6 varieties of potatoes – one waxy and one floury for each first early, second early and main crop but we only grow about 10 tubers of each (yes, OK, that's still a lot of potatoes!). Some companies sell small bags of potatoes like this, although they are more expensive. Alternatively, you may be able to do some swapping with friends. Not only does this method lead to more variety at the table but also it means you will more quickly find your favourite potato varieties.

Shallots

As for onions, sets are the most reliable way to grow shallots. If grown from seed, each seed produces a single shallot. However, if grown from a set, numerous shallots are produced from each set. There isn't a great deal of difference between varieties only subtle differences in colour, shape, size, yield and flavour. You will probably discover one or two varieties that you particularly like and do well in your conditions.

Whatever you order, make a note of it in your garden planner– the crop, the variety and the company you ordered it from. You will forget whether or not you did actually order shallot sets, for example, or just thought about it. If you have a note you will avoid going out and buying something again by mistake. This will also help you with next year's order when you wonder what the name of that wonderful pea variety was, whether you had any of that tomato variety left over, and how many shallot sets you need to order, for example. You may even want to start a gardener's diary.

Selecting gardening equipment

Most people do already have a selection of useful gardening tools before they decide to grow fruit and vegetables. If however, you are starting from scratch or have only a few things, here is a list of the tools I think are essential or useful.

Wheelbarrow, spade, fork, hoe, rake, 2 watering cans (for balance!), trowel, knife, string, and labels.

Preparing your site

January is the ideal time to sort your site out. Plants (including weeds) are dormant and there is no planting or harvesting to be done. If the ground is uncultivated and rough then the best option is to double dig the whole plot. To do this, dig out a spit of ground a spade width wide and a spade deep and load it into a wheelbarrow. Move the dug out earth to the other end of the bed you are going to dig over. Fork over the bottom of the trench you have just dug then dig out another trench next to it, filling the first trench in as you go with the earth from the second trench. Repeat this until you reach the other side of the bed, then fill in the last trench with the earth you barrowed round from the first trench. As you might imagine, this can be back breaking work, particularly on a damp clay soil. However, in the long run it will save hours of weeding and will have been well worth it. Some people opt instead to rotovate their plots. Rotovators can be expensive to buy, but can be hired, and using one is also hard work, though it is usually completed quicker. Even if you are rotovating, you will need to at least clear the plot of large weeds first, because even a rotovator will find it difficult to chop its way through a mat of weeds. Whatever method you use, it is well worth spending the time initially clearing the plot properly, even if that means you only clear a small area in the first year. It is worth noting, however, that there will be times when it is impossible to do anything to your plot because of the weather. Not only will you feel disinclined to go out when the weather is foul, but your soil will be unworkable anyway. It may well be frozen, or too soggy and heavy to dig.

Once the plot is clear you need to mark out the beds and decide where the paths will be. It is then essential that you stick to these paths and avoid walking on the beds. If the beds become compacted under foot you will have to re-dig the area. If you have your hard landscaping to hand then lay this down at this point. You might want to ask your local carpet warehouse if they have any carpet scraps they would be willing to donate – most do! Do please, however, avoid using foam-backed carpet as the foam quickly breaks down and spreads itself around your plot.

Your site is now ready for planting.

Useful things to save

Start collecting useful containers – jars, large yoghurt pots, vegetable trays, polystyrene cups. Although it is possible to buy purpose made preserving jars, such as Kilner jars, I find this unnecessary for your own use. Saved jars are useful for all sorts of pickling and preserving and it is handy to have a variety of different shapes and sizes. The best ones are those with "safety buttons" on the lids. Don't forget bottles too, such as ketchup bottles or sauce bottles. Collect mustard jars if you fancy herb mustard in a few months. It is best to use jam and honey jars for jams; pasta sauce and pickle jars for pickles and so on. It is very important that the jars used are properly cleaned. If you have a dishwasher, clean them in this, or thoroughly by hand in very hot (boiling, even) water and remove their labels. Please clean them properly or you could give yourself a bout of food poisoning! Once dry, store them with their lids on to keep them clean and to keep the lids with the jars. You will never completely get rid of the smell of strongly flavoured foods such as sauces for meat or pickles, so that is why is it best to use them again for something of a similar type. The size and shape of the jar is also convenient for portion size and serving its contents. Large yoghurt pots are only useful if they have re-sealable lids but they can be used for freezing things in, particularly ice cream. Collect pie cases too if you fancy homemade pies later in the year. Foil pie containers are fine. Polystyrene cups and smaller yoghurt pots are useful as plant pots but don't forget to put drainage holes in the bottom. It is best to make drainage holes with something sharp rather than melting a hole as this releases noxious fumes. The trays that pre-packed vegetables come in are handy to use as small seed trays if they have drainage holes put in them, or they can be used to collect and store soft fruit in.

Subsequent Years
Once your plot is established, the jobs for January will be quite different.

Things to do
Continue the winter clear up. Clear away weeds, fork over the soil, wash pots and clean labels. You may also need to do some path maintenance. Carpet paths may well have moss and grass growing on them that needs scraping off. If you used a temporary surface, such as cardboard, this will have disintegrated by now and will need replacing either now or when the weather improves – however, you may have a surplus of cardboard from Christmas that you could use!

Things to expect

Broccoli
Winter broccoli should be growing well by now and may be flowering depending on the variety, its location and the weather.

Carrots and potatoes
Any root-type crops that you harvest now will be damaged, most likely with slug holes, and will probably have other insects living inside the holes such as woodlice.

Fruit
Fruit bushes should have visible, healthy leaf buds.

Onions and Garlic
Autumn sown onions and garlic should be showing signs of life now. The onions will either have green shoots or will be visibly damaged (rotted or eaten) or there will be a space where it should be. Make a note of the number of spaces and decide whether you need to order new onion sets to fill the spaces in the spring. Sadly, there isn't a lot you can do about failed garlic at this stage, although they do sometimes spring into life suddenly later on so don't give up hope.

Things to harvest
Beetroot (late variety).
Broccoli (possibly, depending on variety)
Carrots (will be damaged)
Kale
Leeks
Oriental leaves
Parsnips

Potatoes (will be damaged)
Spinach

Harvesting Tips:
Beetroot
Remove leaves from any beetroot still in the ground to stop the leaves rotting and damaging the roots while they stand. Don't expect them to grow any larger now - if they are small pick them now for pickling as whole baby beets.

In storage
Frozen fruit and vegetables
Garlic
Miscellaneous jarred preserves
Onions
Potatoes
Shallots

In the Kitchen

Pickled whole baby beets

Ingredients
Golf-ball sized beetroots
Pickling or malt vinegar (see Equipment and Techniques chapter)

Equipment
Saucepan, knife, jar and lid, and greaseproof paper.

Method
Twist off the tops of the beetroot and scrub clean. Do not peel or remove the top or trailing part of the root as this causes them to bleed into the cooking water. Place in a saucepan and cover with boiling water from a kettle. Bring back to the boil and simmer for about half an hour. Drain and allow to cool slightly so they can be handled. With your fingers, rub off the skin and root. Don't worry about getting red fingers because it washes off easily. Cut off tops and bottoms and drop the roots into a jar whilst still warm. Use a suitable sized jar so that it is well packed with beetroots. Pour over the pickling vinegar until the beets are covered. Add a piece of scrunched up greaseproof paper to the neck of the jar to help keep the beetroot submerged beneath the vinegar. Screw on the lid and label.

Storage
Store for 2 to 3 months to allow flavours to develop, consume within the year.

Usage
To accompany cold meat, or as part of a salad.

Mashed potato with cheese

Whether you are eating potatoes out of your store or still digging them up, they will be "old" potatoes and probably a little bit worse for wear (beginning to sprout or slug damaged). So one of the best ways to deal with tatty potatoes is to mash them. Below is a delicious mashed potato recipe that really makes the most out of otherwise poor quality spuds. If you have the time and energy, now is a good time to make large batches of mashed potato to freeze. Stored potatoes will deteriorate from now on, especially once they start sprouting, and will become shrivelled and soft. So, if you mash them now and freeze them you will preserve your spuds as well as have a ready supply of convenient, quick mashed potato. This type of mash is particularly good if used as the topping on a shepherd's pie or fish pie, or as the basis for potato cakes, so freeze it in convenient sized portions. I do warn you though that all that mashing does require quite a lot of energy! You could use a food processor, of course, but many people dislike the creamed texture that produces.

Ingredients (serves 2)
Potatoes
Knob of butter
1 tablespoon olive oil
1 tablespoon milk
Salt and Pepper
Cheese

Equipment
Potato peeler, knife, saucepan, masher, cheese grater, bowl, ovenproof dish (approximately 20 by 15 cm), fish slice or spatula.

Method
Peel the potatoes and cut into small chucks (2 by 2 cm). Place in a pan and cover with boiling water from the kettle. Add salt to the water and bring back to the boil. Simmer for about 10 minutes until the potatoes are soft. Drain the potatoes over a large bowl so that the hot

water warms the bowl then discard the water except for about 1 dessert spoon's worth – retaining as much of the potato starch as possible. Tip the potatoes into the bowl and add the butter, oil and milk, adjusting the quantities if necessary to avoid the potatoes becoming too sloppy (this will vary depending on the potato variety used). Season to taste. Preheat a grill. Mash these ingredients together then beat the potatoes to remove any remaining lumps. Transfer the mash to the ovenproof dish and smooth level. Grate over a thin layer of cheese (you might also like to add a few drops of soy or Worcestershire sauce for extra flavour) and place under the grill for 2 to 3 minutes until the cheese has melted and is slightly brown. Divide into 2 portions with a fish slice and remove from the dish in 2 blocks to serve.

Usage
As a side dish to any meal.

Variations
To make leek and cheese mashed potato, wash and cut a leek into rounds about half a centimetre thick. Boil in lightly salted water at the same time as you are cooking the potatoes. Drain once soft (approximately 10 minutes), reserving about 2 teaspoons worth of water. Add the water and the leeks to the potatoes once mashed and combine, then proceed as before.

To make swede and cheese mashed potato, substitute some of the potato for swede but treat it in the same way. This makes a surprisingly tasty, slightly golden coloured mash and is a good way to get children to eat a portion of veg.

Fish Pie

Ingredients (serves 1 or 2)
10 oz (280 g) potatoes
1 haddock fillet (or other fish of your choosing, e.g. try smoked fish or salmon)
1 tbsp olive oil or milk
Salt and pepper
1 medium carrot
1 clove garlic
1 small piece of root ginger
Knob of butter or 1 tbsp olive oil
Milk

1 oz prawns
2 tsp tartare sauce
Cheese
Worstershire sauce (optional)

Equipment
2 saucepans, 2 plates, knife, bowl, potato masher, ovenproof dish and grater.

Method
Preheat oven to 200 °C, 400 °F, gas mark 6. Peel and chop the potato into small chunks and put them in a pan of lightly salted, boiling water. Bring back to the boil then simmer for 10 minutes. Place a plate over the pan as it boils and place the fish onto it. Season with salt and pepper (or fish seasoning, see September) and pour oil or milk over the fish to moisten. Cover with another plate and steam for 10 minutes whilst the potatoes cook. In the meantime, peel and chop the carrots and boil. Chop the garlic and ginger into fine pieces. When ready, drain the potatoes over a bowl and discard all the water expect for about 1 tablespoon worth which should be rich in potato starch. Season and add butter or oil. Mash until smooth, adding milk if necessary. Pull or cut the fish from skin and discard the skin. Add the prawns, garlic, ginger, tartare sauce and seasoning. Combine well then spoon into the bottom of a suitable ovenproof dish. Layer the carrots over the fish then spoon the mashed potatoes over the top and spread out evenly. Grate cheese over the potato and add the Worcestershire sauce if using. Bake in the centre of the oven for 20-25 minutes until the cheese has browned and the pie is hot through.

Storage
The fish pie can be frozen before grating the cheese over the potato. To cook, defrost thoroughly and cook at 190 °C, 375 °F, gas mark 5 for 25 to 30 minutes, or cook from frozen for 35 to 40 minutes. Check the pie is thoroughly warm before serving.

Usage
Serves 1 as a complete meal or 2 with suitable accompaniment.

February

February is probably the slackest time of year on the plot. You will probably be impatient to get things started but the weather at this time of year will make it difficult to do much on the plot itself. However, things are beginning to happen slowly and you can make a start.

First Year

Things to do

Cloches
Cloches are any type of small, protective covering you put over plants to give them extra warmth. There is a whole range of different types of cloches, made from different materials, ranging from the homemade to the very expensive. To get your vegetable growing off to a good start you will ideally need some sort of cloche so this month is a good time to either start making some or to order some. The very simplest type of cloche is one made from large plastic bottles. I would recommend using clear plastic bottles of 2 litres capacity or more, preferably originally containing a liquid which is easy to wash out (i.e. not cooking oil!). Using a sharp knife and some care, cut off the bottom of the bottle and remove its lid. Each bottle will cover one small plant, such as a broad bean plant, just long enough to get it established. By the time the plant touches the sides of the bottle it should be established enough for you to remove it and allow it to fend for itself and you can move it to another needy plant.

Agricultural fleece is another good way of protecting plants. This keeps plants warm but also allows some light and water to pass through it. In its simplest form, you can loosely lay a sheet of fleece over an area of crops and weight it or peg it down. It is also possible to buy fleece (or plastic) already made into small tunnel shapes that can be used on individual rows. These are quite expensive and you may find that their size is inappropriate for your plot for one reason or another. I was fortunate enough to be given a large sheet of fleece and some flexible poles as a gift and I spent one February day cutting the fleece to size and sowing in sleeves for the poles. I now have 6 custom-made fleece tunnels that perfectly fit the width of my seedbeds.

Pieces of glass, such as old windows also make good cloches, especially if they can be secured into a convenient shape, such as an

A-frame. However, they should not be used if the glass has sharp edges or if children are likely to injure themselves on them.

There are also many other designs of cloches that can be bought ranging from plastic sheeting to glass bell jars. Your choice of cloches will depend on your budget, your resources and your needs. You may even decide that you don't initially need cloches and certainly the more straightforward crops can be grow successfully without them and even the more tender crops can be grown without them but are more of a gamble.

Cold frames
Some people have conservatories, potting sheds or greenhouses that they can put tender plants in. However, I have never had these luxuries and it certainly wouldn't be reasonable of me to suggest a huge expense of a greenhouse to you either. Thus, this book is keyed for growing everything outside. Nevertheless, I couldn't manage without a cold frame. These are small-unheated structures, rather like a large cloche. There are a variety of designs and a range of prices. Some are designed to go over a seedbed and some are free-standing. I recommend you spend about 20 or 30 pounds at *Argos* or at your local garden centre buying a small free-standing plastic cold frame. These are a three or four-tiered shelving unit, covered in a clear, flexible plastic coat with zips for access. This piece of equipment will become invaluable later on so it is worth buying now.

Every Year

Things to Do

Garlic
I have always found that garlic is much more likely to succeed if it is planted in the autumn. This is probably because it needs to be exposed to cold to set it growing. However, it is possible to have garlic grow successfully if planted at this time of year and a neat trick is to put the bulbs in the fridge for a few days before planting. Divide a bulb up into it cloves and plant each clove as you would for an onion set.

Leeks
It is also possible to sow leeks at this time of year. They don't need light to germinate and can cope with fairly low temperatures too. I find they germinate fine inside my garage but it is important to remove them to a position of light as soon as they emerge so that they can grow on. If you have space in your cold frame put them in there.

Onions and Shallots

You may find that your onion or shallot sets arrive this month. If the weather really is awful then it is best to store the sets in a cool dry place until things improve. If you plant them out in soggy, cold soil, not only will it be a very unpleasant experience but they will be more prone to rotting too. If the weather is reasonable (for February!) then plant them out now. I find using a dibber is best and just push them into the ground up to their necks. Some people do completely bury their sets simply because birds tend to think that the top of a set is a worm and pull it out of the ground. I do find this happens to one or two but they can be pushed back in again without much harm. To be honest, I used to dread planting onion and shallot sets. It can be a backbreaking job in very unpleasant conditions. It is difficult to wear gloves because it is fiddly and wet, and whether you do or not, your hands become numb – and your feet too! I now get around this problem by buying autumn sowing onion sets to plant in October, and heat-treated onion and shallot sets that don't have to be planted until March or April when conditions are considerably better. The only disadvantages of this are that they tend to be slightly more expensive and they need to be planted at a time when you will be very busy with sowing other things. Leaving this job to March is perfectly fine as long as you have somewhere suitable (cool, dry and frost-free) to store the bulbs until ready.

Potatoes

You may also find that your seed potatoes arrive at this time of year. It used to be the case that seed potatoes were kept in cold storage until March before being dispatched to the customer or garden centre. However, they are now sent out at or just after Christmas, supposedly to give you time to chit your potatoes but probably most likely so that they don't take up the merchant's valuable space later when other things, such as bulbs, can be sold. Chitting potatoes means allowing them to grow short, sturdy green shoots and is supposed to give your potatoes a good start and to provide an earlier crop. This means they need to be arranged in a single layer and left out in a light, frost-free place.

If you wish to chit your potatoes you should firstly check over your seed potatoes as you may have the occasional tuber that is rotting and this needs to be disposed of. The next problem you will have is how to set them up for chitting and where to put them so that they get enough light and are kept free from frost. Some people use egg boxes to put the potatoes in and put them on their windowsills. This is fine if you only have a few potatoes, have reasonable sized windowsills and don't mind having potatoes sat on them for a month. However, I use my cold frame and locate it outside in a sheltered but sunny position. I have it in a corner on a south-facing wall. Ideally, you want it to get plenty of light during the day but remain frost-free at night. Apart from in very severe cold weather, the warmth of a wall should help to keep it free from frost. It is also worth finding something heavy to weight it down with so that the wind or cats can't knock it over. Then simply lay your seed potatoes in shallow cardboard boxes (such as the fruit and vegetable boxes from supermarkets), and put them inside the cold frame and zip it closed. It is necessary to unzip the cold frame on a sunny day, however, otherwise you could end up with baked seed potatoes!

You may well decide that you do not wish to chit your potatoes. Certainly there is some debate as to whether it is, at best, necessary and, at worst, detrimental. A slightly early crop of new potatoes may well be beneficial to commercial growers but makes little difference to the home grower. Once a potato is chitted, its internal clock is started and if it spends time growing before being planted then it could potentially reduce the overall yield. So, it is possible that chitting is useful for an early crop of new potatoes but unnecessary for second early or main crop potatoes. However, you will need to keep your seed potatoes dark and cool but frost-free (4-5 °C; 40 °F) to stop them sprouting and producing long, white shoots if you decide not to chit. Again, it is worth checking them over for any rotting tubers that could spread rot to adjacent potatoes. If you cannot guarantee these conditions (i.e. you don't have suitable refrigeration facilities!) it may be safer to chit them just to prevent them being damaged either by frost or from producing leggy shoots.

Subsequent Years

Things to do

Winter clear up and fruit maintenance
Finish the winter clear up, including pruning apple and pear tree and fruit bushes. Delay this task if the temperature is likely to be below freezing as frost can damage newly cut wood. Retain any large pieces of pruned twigs to use later on as "pea-sticks".

Things to harvest

Carrots (just)
Kale
Leeks
Oriental leaves
Parsnip
Purple sprouting broccoli
Spinach
White sprouting broccoli

In Storage

Frozen fruit and vegetables
Garlic
Miscellaneous jarred preserves
Onions
Potatoes
Shallots

Onions, shallots, garlic and potatoes might all start sprouting this month. If this happens, use these first as they will quickly deteriorate.

In the Kitchen

Chicken and Leek Casserole

It seems to me that vegetables are in season at just the point when you most want to eat them. Winter vegetables, such as leeks and roots are ideal for making filling winter casseroles that are wonderful to eat on a cold night, and salad crops are perfect as a light summer meal!

Ingredients (serves 2)
Cooking oil (for frying)
2 skinned and boned chicken breasts
1 or 2 leeks (depending on size)
2 - 3 carrots (and/or parsnip/swede)
½ pint (250 ml) of stock
3 – 5 potatoes
2 –3 sprigs of sage, thyme and rosemary
2 –3 bay leaves
1 large garlic clove (optional)

Salt and pepper

Equipment
Large deep frying pan, potato peeler, tongs, spatula, knife, large spoon and casserole dish (without lid)

Method
To prepare vegetables:
Wash the leeks and remove the outer layer. Top and tail and wash away any soil between the layers then cut them into rounds. Wash and peel carrots and cut into rounds. Wash and peel potatoes and cut into rounds. Remove herb leaves from their stalks and discard any tough stems then tear the leaves into pieces. Peel and finely chop the garlic.

To prepare casserole:
Preheat oven to 190 °C, 375 °F, gas mark 5. Heat some oil in a frying plan then add the chicken breasts. Fry for 5 to 8 minutes until brown all over. Lift from the pan and set aside. Add the leeks and carrots and fry for 3 to 4 minutes. Return the chicken to the pan, and add the stock, potatoes, herbs and garlic. Season and bring to the boil. Transfer the chicken, leeks and carrots to the casserole dish and layer the potatoes on top so that they cover the meat and vegetables. Place in the oven and cook for 40 to 50 minutes until the top layer of potatoes is brown and crisp.

Usage
Serves 2 for a very filling winter meal.

Leek Stock

Ingredients
2 – 3 leeks
Water
Salt

Equipment
Saucepan, clean jar (ideally with a "safety button")

Method
Wash the leeks, top and tail and cut into rounds. Add the leeks to the saucepan and cover with water. Salt, and bring to the boil. Simmer for

about 10 minutes.   Drain the water into the clean jar and seal immediately. Serve the leeks with a meal.

Storage
Once the stock has cooled the safety button should have become depressed again. If it has, then the stock can be stored for several months, if not then use within 3 days.

Usage
In any recipe requiring stock.

To make tasty gravy: crumble 1 stock cube into a saucepan and add 2 tsp of plain flour. Add a tbsp cold water and make into a paste or smooth batter. Add the stock and heat until gravy boils and thickens.

March

March is when it all starts to happen and you can finally get on with growing some crops. However, if the weather is very wet, be patient and delay doing anything. Planting in unsuitable conditions is not only miserable for you but for the plants too and they will suffer if they get very cold and wet.

First year

Things to do

Herbs
March is a good time to think about your herb garden. Perhaps the easiest and quickest way to establish a herb garden is to pop down to your local garden centre and buy in some suitable plants. Remember, however, to leave some space for tender annual herbs, such as basil. A cheaper, and perhaps more satisfying, way to do it is to grow your own herbs from seeds. Most herbs can be grown easily from seeds with a few exceptions such as lemon thyme, bay, fennel and tarragon. Now is a good time to sow hardy herbs such as rosemary and savory. They will need to be sown in a heated propagator at this time of year or put on a warm windowsill with plastic over them. Most herbs originate from a Mediterranean climate so like full sun, well drained soil and can tolerate drought. All are suitable for pot growing.

There are, of course, hundreds of plants that come under the general name of herb. There are fewer, but still numerous, which can be classified as culinary herbs. Deciding which herbs to grow can be difficult. Here is a brief, and by no means exhaustive, guide to the herbs you may consider.

Basil
This herb is essential for tomato dishes. There is a huge range of variation in basil plants, from unusual appearance to different flavours, but all can be grown easily from seed. It is a tender annual and can only be grown outdoors from June to October. It can be grown in pots inside, although it will get leggy if it doesn't have enough light. It is worth growing more than one plant and several varieties so that there is always plenty to hand. It has a pretty white, pink or purple flower but the quality of the leaves diminish whilst it is flowering. Interesting varieties to consider are purple basil, Thai basil and lemon basil.

Bay

Although not directly edible, bay is an essential flavouring to add to stocks, soups, sauces and casseroles. Bay needs to be bought as a plant. It will eventually grow into a large bush or tree but it is slow growing and easily trained. It is a woody herb but is vulnerable to severe frosts and needs to be situated in a sheltered position. It is a perennial evergreen. Although it does flower, the flowers are white and fairly insignificant.

Chives

Chives give dishes a subtle slightly onion flavour. They are easy to grow from seed and grow rapidly to form clumps that self seed and spread. They have a grass like appearance but produce beautiful purple pom-pom flowers. They can be propagated by division. They are a perennial evergreen. A useful variation is the garlic chive, which has a much more garlicky flavour to it than the conventional chive. Its leaves are flatter and it produces a white flower. It is slightly slower growing and less likely to spread.

Fennel

This is best bought as a plant and has two main variants – standard green and bronze. The bronze fennel is slightly more attractive but otherwise behaves in the same way as the green. If you buy a small fennel plant it is easy to underestimate how tall it will grow. Give the plant plenty of space because it will grow to about 5 ft in a season. It has attractive fern-like foliage and produces tiny yellow flowers. It dies back every winter and the dead wood needs to be cut back. It then regrows all 5 ft the next year. Both the leaves and the seeds can be used in a variety of dishes and have an aniseed flavour.

Lemon balm

This is an attractive herb with a strange lemon flavour to it, rather reminiscent of washing up liquid. It is a hardy, woody perennial evergreen that can be harvested all year round.

Mint

There are numerous varieties of mints, with different appearances and subtly different flavours. Some can be grown successfully from seed whilst others should be bought as plants. Mint is an invasive plant that will quickly spread and swamp neighbours if not controlled. The easiest way to control mint is to keep it confined to a pot, even if the pot is then sunk in the ground. It is still important to keep an eye out for escaping runners. Mint can suffer from rust, which makes it inedible. It is a hardy, woody perennial evergreen that can be harvested most of the year and can be propagated from cuttings.

Oregano and Marjoram
I have grouped these two together because they are very similar. If you have limited space then you need only grow one or the other of these. They are both useful herbs in "Italian" dishes such as pasta sauces and pizzas and go very well with tomatoes. There are both annual and perennial varieties of these and clearly it is more economical in the long run to look for the perennials. Both come in either standard green or golden varieties, with the golden being slightly more attractive to grow.

Parsley
This is a popular herb and now comes in two main varieties – curly and flat leaf. Both are biennial and will flower then die in its second year so it needs to be replaced often. It can be grown readily from seeds and is used in a variety of dishes as both flavouring and a garnish.

Rosemary
This to me seems to be an essential herb that goes particularly well with red meats such as lamb and beef but which has numerous other uses in the kitchen. It can be sown successfully from seed, although it is relatively slow growing in the first few years and you may decide to buy an established plant to get things going quickly. It has attractive pink/purple flowers but it may not flower readily. It is a hardy, woody, perennial evergreen that can be harvested all year round and can be propagated from cuttings.

Sage
Sage seems to be another essential herb that goes well with pork, game and poultry. There are numerous variations of sage plants with different leaf patterns and subtly different flavours. The straightforward green variety can be grown readily from seed and will grow quickly. Other variations are best bought as plants and tend to be slightly more fragile. Of the variations I would recommend getting a purple sage if you have room for more than one sage plant. This is a very attractive plant to have in the garden as well as in recipes. It is fast growing and as tolerate as the green variety. It also has the advantage that it doesn't tend to flower, so as the green variety is busy looking beautiful with its spectacular purple flowers, the purple variety is still happily producing top quality leaves. Sage is a hardy, woody perennial evergreen that can be harvested all year round and can be propagated from cuttings.

Savory

This has an unusual flavour but it is an excellent companion for broad beans. It has a low growing habit and produces small, surprisingly sharp leaves and white flowers. It can be grown from seed. It is a hardy, woody perennial evergreen that can be harvested all year round and can be propagated from cuttings.

Tarragon

This is best bought as a plant. It is a woody plant that dies back completely in the winter but regrows the following year. It has an unusual flavour that seems to especially suit fish dishes.

Thyme

Thyme is a useful culinary herb that goes well with most meat and in other dishes. Its small leaves and woody stems can make it a bit fiddly to use, as the leaves have to be stripped from the stems before they can be used. It is low growing and makes an excellent edging plant. It is relatively slow growing so more than one plant is probably useful. It flowers with attractive small white, pink or purple flowers. There are numerous variations of thyme with different leaves and flavours. Standard thyme can be grown successfully from seed but variations are best bought as plants. Of the variations, the most useful I find is lemon thyme. This has an attractive yellow variegation and an unmistakable lemon scent. It retains its lemon flavour on cooking and drying and is excellent with fish and home-made salad dressings. Thyme is a hardy, woody perennial evergreen that can be harvested all year round and can be propagated from cuttings.

Fruit

Although most fruit should be planted during the autumn and winter, strawberries can be planted in March and April. They are very easy plants to grow and you will probably have to thin your plants in the future to keep them under control. They need very little special treatment, although some people like to surround the plants with a layer of straw or special strawberry matting to keep the fruit clean as it forms. Others like to net against birds but if you do this, make sure you wait until after the flowers have been pollinated or use netting coarse enough to let bees through.

Every year

Things to do

Broad beans

Broad beans can be sown directly into the soil at this time of year but I find a much better germination and success rate is attained if they are started inside in pots and then planted out by the end of the month under cloches. It is important to only grow the plants inside for 2 weeks or less or else they become leggy and weak and struggle once outside. Germination will take a week or two so ideally sow at the beginning of the month but don't worry if you don't manage it for some reason as they soon catch up. I sow one bean per pot (a pot being anything from a polystyrene coffee cup or a small yoghurt pot to a small plastic flowerpot). Place them in a bright position such as a sunny window sill until germinated then put them out in the cold frame to harden off once they have emerged. The cold frame will have better light than a windowsill anyway so will lessen the chances of it becoming leggy, and the cooler conditions will help the plant acclimatise before being planted out. Plant out when 3 to 6 inches (7 – 15 cm) tall and place a bottle cloche over each plant if you have them. This helps to protect them from the cold, from slugs and from the leaf cutter beetle until they are more established. Protect the whole crop from slugs, particularly if the conditions are damp.

Carrots, beetroot and parsnips

These too can potentially be grown outside at this time of year but germination rates are low, particularly for parsnips and it can just be a waste of seed. If any do manage to germinate then slugs and snails will most likely eat them before you even set eyes on them. Again, patience is required – wait till next month.

First Early Potatoes

Now is also the time to plant your first early potato sets. If they have been chitting for a month (see February) they should have some nice, short, dark green shoots. These can be knocked off very easily so take care when handling them. First early potatoes can be planted slightly closer together than main crop because they are harvested when smaller, so if you are short of space you can plant them 5 inches (12 cm) deep, 8 inches (20 cm) apart and with 18 inches (45 cm) between rows. If you have well rotten compost or manure then stick some of that in with them. Not only does it help the plants to grow but also it seems to offer some protection from slugs and, surprisingly, the tubers come out of the ground cleaner. If you only have a limited amount of this then save it for your main crop potatoes which will benefit more from its fertilising and protection properties. If you have fleece or clear plastic then protect the potatoes with it as it helps get them off to a good start and protects emerging foliage from frost; if not then pack newspaper around emerging shoots if frost is forecast.

Leeks
Sow leeks in pots if you didn't manage it last month or pot on your leeks sown last month if they are big enough.

Onions, shallots and garlic
If you didn't get these planted last month then get them in now.

Peas
It is possible to sow peas outside at this time of year but, again, success rates will be lower. This is partly to do with the cold, damp condition of the soil and partly because creatures such as mice and birds enjoy the seeds to fill their hungry gap. My advice is to wait until next month.

Watercress
For years I avoided growing this because I was repeatedly told that it wouldn't grow unless next to a source of running water, such as a stream, which, naturally, I didn't have. However, it is in fact relatively easy to grow in poorly drained containers kept in a shady position. The key seems to be a lack of drainage and constantly damp (though not stagnant) soil. So, if you want to give it a go, sow some seeds in a suitable container this month and place on a windowsill until they germinates.

Subsequent years

Things to do

Brassicas
Continue harvesting kale regularly or it will start to bolt – watch out for a sudden gain in height as a sign of bolting.

Fruit
Finish pruning woody fruit plants this month.

Herbs
March is a good time to take cuttings from woody herbs such as rosemary, sage and thyme for propagation.

Things to expect

Blossom on plum, cherry and peach trees. Be prepared to throw fleece over the tree to protect the blossom if frost is forecast, as losing the blossom will reduce the fruit yield.

Things to harvest

Kale
Leeks
Oriental leaves
Parsnips
Purple sprouting broccoli
White sprouting broccoli

Finish harvesting leeks by the end of the month as they will bolt during April and become inedible.

Harvesting Tips

Broccoli
Unlike conventional "broccoli" (calebrese), true 'sprouting' broccoli does not form one large central head. Instead it forms numerous small shoots that are either purple or a light green or white, depending on the variety. To harvest, simply snap or cut off each flowering shoot, retaining an inch or two of the stem which is also quite edible. The shoots should be harvested when the flower is still tightly in bud. If the bud begins to open then still remove the shoot but discard it. It is important to check the plants at least once a week because if the flowers open then it will stop producing new buds and your crop will finish.

Cooking Tips

Broccoli
Broccoli does not require much cooking. Either boil it in lightly salted water for 3 to 5 minutes until tender, or steam (see Equipment and Techniques chapter).

In Storage

Frozen fruit and vegetables
Garlic
Miscellaneous jarred preserves
Onions

Potatoes
Shallots

Your stored bulbs and tubers will really begin to sprout now and may become inedible. Now might be a good time to make and freeze mashed potato (see January)

In the kitchen

Broccoli and Salmon Quiche

Ingredients (Serves 4-6)
For base:
4 oz (110 g) plain flour
4 oz (110 g) wholemeal flour (alternatively use a total of 8 oz plain flour)
4 oz (110 g) margarine or butter
Pinch of salt

For filling:
8 oz (225 g) broccoli
2 oz (55 g) smoked salmon
2 eggs
6 fl oz (170 ml) skimmed or semi-skimmed milk
Freshly ground black pepper
Herbs (optional) such as lemon thyme or tarragon

Equipment
Two bowls (large and small), sieve, rolling pin, 1 × 9 inch flan dish or 2 × 5 inch flan dishes, knife, saucepan, scissors, fork.

Method
Preheat oven to 200 °C, 400 °F, gas mark 6. Sift flours and salt into a bowl, including any bran that remains in the sieve. Add the diced fat and rub in until the mixture resembles fine breadcrumbs. Add enough cold water to bind the mixture together and form a firm dough ball. Roll the pastry out onto a lightly floured surface and use it to line a 9-inch (23 cm) or two 5-inch (12 cm) greased flan dishes. Blind bake for 10-15 minutes. Reduce oven temperature to 190 °C, 375 °F, gas mark 5. Roughly chop the broccoli and boil in lightly salted water until just tender. Drain well and arrange it in the bottom of the flan case(s). Snip the smoked salmon into small pieces with scissors and arrange over the broccoli. In another bowl beat together the eggs and the milk

and add the pepper and herbs if using. Pour the mixture over the broccoli and salmon so that it is covered. Bake for about 40 minutes (less if using 2 dishes) until set. Test with a fork, which should come away clean if it is cooked.

Storage
Can be kept in the refrigerator for up to three days and reheated in the microwave or oven.

Usage
Serve hot or cold as a snack, as the basis of a main meal with potatoes and vegetables, or in small slices as finger food.

Broccoli with Garlic Dressing

Ingredients
Broccoli shoots (enough for 2 servings)
3 cloves garlic
2 tablespoons olive oil
Pinch salt
2 tablespoons water
Freshly ground black pepper

Equipment
Knife, saucepan and/or steamer, frying pan, spatula.

Method
Wash the broccoli and cut it into small florets. Steam it for 3 to 5 minutes until tender. Heat the oil in a frying pan over a medium heat. Finely chop or crush the garlic. When the oil is hot, add the salt, then the garlic and sauté, stirring frequently, for 1 to 2 minutes until the garlic starts to soften. Quickly add the water and the pepper. Turn down the heat to low and simmer for a couple of minutes. Pour the garlic mixture over the broccoli and mix gently to coat and serve hot.

Storage
Any leftovers can be stored in the refrigerator overnight and served cold in a salad the next day.

Usage
As a starter or a side dish.

Broccoli and Salmon Risotto

Ingredients
Oil (for frying)
1 medium onion
1 garlic clove
4¾ oz (140g) risotto rice
1¼ pints (700 ml) fish stock (see Equipment and Techniques chapter)
5 oz (150g) broccoli
1¾ oz (50g) smoked salmon
1 salmon fillet
Salt and pepper

Equipment
Knife, large frying pan, spatula, saucepan.

Method
Finely chop the onions and garlic. Dice both types of salmon. Heat the oil in a large frying pan and fry the onion until soft. Add the garlic and rice and stir for 1 to 2 minutes to coat the rice well. Add the fish stock, stirring so that rice absorbs the stock and continue to simmer, stirring occasionally. In the meantime, blanch the broccoli for 1 minute in boiling water. When the rice is almost cooked, add the two types of salmon and the broccoli and season. Cook for a further 5 minutes and serve immediately.

Usage
As a meal for 2.

April

April is a very busy month in the garden but still very lean in the kitchen.

First year

Things to do

Asparagus
Asparagus in a perennial crop that will keep on going for many years. However, it requires patience because it takes several years to become established before you can start to harvest it. If you wish to grow asparagus, the most successful method is to plant 1 year old asparagus crowns. It is possible to grow asparagus from seed but this further delays the time it takes before you get your first harvest. It is essential that you choose your site well as it will be in it for a long time (possibly 15 to 20 years) and you don't want it in the way or in a poor situation. It is also important to prepare the bed well, removing all weeds and adding sharp sand if necessary so that it is well drained. It may also be advantageous to grow the crowns on small mounds to aid drainage. This is an occasion when you have to check your tenancy agreement if you are renting an allotment as asparagus may be forbidden if you are not allowed to plant perennial crops.

Fruit
If you wish to grow a grapevine then April is the month to plant it. Make sure it is planted somewhere sheltered with good drainage and that you provide adequate support.

Herbs
If growing herbs from seeds then all types can be sown at this time of the year in pots, protected by polythene.

Every year

Things to do

Broad beans
Plant out any beans grown in pots if you have not already done. If already done, then check the bean inside bottle cloches and remove the cloches if they have outgrown them. If you have spare seed and space, broad beans can now be sown directly in the soil. Re-establish slug protection measures around beans and new sowings.

Carrots, beetroot and parsnips

These can be sown in drills in a fine tilth. In order to achieve a fine tilth, the seed bed will first have to be dug or forked over and any large lumps broken down. It should then be raked backwards and forwards until it takes on a fine, crumbly texture like breadcrumbs. This is hard work but fine seeds will not germinate if the soil is too lumpy and carrots will fork if the soil is compacted beneath the surface. Pull out a drill with the corner of your hoe, water the base of the drill then scatter the seeds in and recover. If you really are struggling to get a fine tilth then line the base of the drill with potting compost or sand instead and sow into this. It is best to water the base of the drill as this ensures the water is next to the seed where it is needed and if you water the surface it can disturb the seeds and form a hard cap of soil that the seedlings can't break through. These crops certainly need protecting from slugs and may also need protecting from cats if they tend to scratch up your soil.

Onions and Shallots

Heat-treated onion sets will arrive this month and this month is the last opportunity to plant onions and shallots.

Peas and Mangetout

Now is the ideal time to sow peas and mangetout directly in the soil. Remove a shallow trench the width of your hoe and scatter in seeds then cover over with about 1 inch (2.5 cm) of soil. It is a good ideal to put "pea-sticks" in the ground now to support the peas once they start growing. Use any branched twigs available, ideally to a height of about 3 feet. If you don't have suitable twigs, use string between canes or netting.

Potatoes

Plant the second early potatoes at the beginning of the month and the main crops by the end of the month. These need to be planted 6 inches (15 cm) deep, 12 inches (30 cm) apart and with 24 inches (60 cm) between rows. Manure or compost is well worth adding if you have it.

Salad crops

Salad crops can be sown in the same way as the root crops above. These include lettuce, radish, spring onions and rocket. However, you might want to sow only a row of these at a time and wait two weeks before sowing another row so that you have a succession of these crops.

Tender crops

Tender crops are those that cannot survive a frost. These can be sown in pots at this time of the year. They generally need warmth to get them to germinate and lots of light once they start growing. These crops include tomatoes, peppers and aubergines. If you are growing **tomatoes** check that you have chosen outdoor varieties. **Peppers and aubergines** are more of a challenge without a greenhouse and at least need cloche protection. I grow them every year with ample optimism but only sometimes successfully get a crop. It should at least be possible to get small, green peppers if nothing else.

Tender crops also include the cucurbit family – cucumbers, courgettes, gherkins, pumpkins, melons, squashes etc. Outdoor **cucumbers** are very straightforward so should be attempted. If you can't successfully grow a glut of **courgettes** you may as well forget vegetable growing as a hobby! **Gherkins** are also very easy. **Pumpkins** will at least give you rampant foliage but may, occasionally, fail to bear fruit. **Melons** are much more of a challenge and require at least some cloche protection as well as a good summer.

Miscellaneous tender crops include basil, celery, lablab beans and cape gooseberries. I like to grow several sorts of **basil** and treat it as a crop rather than a herb because it is an annual and I grow lots of it. **Celery** is fairly easy to grow but may produce tougher, less flavoursome sticks than those you can buy in supermarkets if you choose an unfortunate variety. Leaf or cutting celery is also a good option as it provides the flavour of celery in tender leaves that are nice in salads and soups. **Lablab** beans (Ruby Moon) are unusual climbing beans with beautiful pink and purple flowers and dark purple, flat pods. These are very attractive plants in their own right which are worth growing for their appearance with the beans as an added bonus. **Cape gooseberries** can be found in the exotic fruit section of supermarkets as Physalis. It is an unusual orange fruit contained within papery husks similar to Chinese lanterns. They make excellent jelly and jam but can frequently fail to produce enough ripe fruit before the frosts.

Things to expect

Asparagus

The spears should emerge this month. Do not cut in the first year. You may decide not to cut in the second year too so that the plants gets well established, however, they will probably stand the removal of a few stems if you really can't wait.

Broad beans
Your broad bean plants should look established if they were planted out last month. If they were unprotected by cloches or the cloches have been removed for a while then the edges of the leaves have probably now been scalloped by the leaf-cutter beetle. This does not seem to affect the crop in any way so no action is needed.

Potatoes
By the end of this month your first early potatoes should have started to sprout above the surface of the soil. If frost is forecast, protect new shoots with fleece, straw, newspaper or by covering over with soil.

Soil
Your soil at this time of year will probably be at its most workable. It will still be damp but not soggy so it should be easy to dig, break into a tilth and rake.

Subsequent years

Things to do

Asparagus
There is an old wife's tale that says that asparagus benefits from a dressing of salt at this time of year. It is true that asparagus was originally a coastal plant and can thus tolerate saltier conditions than most plants. However, the main benefit seems to be that the salt does not harm the asparagus but makes it more difficult for weeds and fungus to grow, therefore protecting the asparagus. If you wish to apply salt, do so at a rate of 1½ oz per sq yd (50 g per m^2)

Herbs
Divide large clumps of herbs such as lemon balm, fennel and chives to stop them from taking over and to provide new plants.

Things to expect

Brassicas
Brassicas tend to get attacked by aphids at this time of year, particularly blackfly on the broccoli. Chances are that it will not do much harm before the crop is over so, apart from squashing what you can see, no action is necessary.

Fruit
Currant bushes should now be in leaf and may also have developed some very insignificant flowers.

Peach trees will probably have developed leaf curl – remove affected leaves. Strawberries, apples and pears should now be in blossom.

Things to harvest
Asparagus
Celery
Leeks
Oriental leaves
Parsnips
Purple sprouting broccoli
Spinach
White sprouting broccoli

The broccoli will be on its last legs by now. The leeks, parsnips and oriental leaves will bolt during this month so eat them while you can. By the time they bolt you should have some asparagus to harvest.

In storage
Your potatoes and onions will now probably have sprouted so much they will be soft and inedible. Discard any stored produce that is unfit to eat and resort to eating up your frozen and preserved produce. You will need the freezer space by June anyway, and remember to keep and clean jars as you empty them.

Harvesting tips

Asparagus
Use a sharp knife to cut 4 - 5 inch (10 – 13 cm) spears off just below soil level.

Cooking tips

Asparagus
The best way to cook asparagus is to steam it (see Equipment and Techniques chapter). Wash the spears and remove any hard stem. Place in a steamer and steam for 5 to 10 minutes until tender. Serve with a little salt and pepper and butter or olive oil. Ideal as a starter or as a side dish.

Celery Soup

Celery is a biennial crop so should survive the winter but then flower and die. This soup is a useful way to use up any of last year's celery before it goes to seed.

Ingredients (serves 4)
1 small head of celery (and/or leaf celery)
1 medium onion
1 garlic clove
3 sprigs parsley
2 bay leaves
1 sprig thyme
1 pint (600 ml) stock (chicken or vegetable)
1 oz (25 g) flour
Pinch of grated nutmeg
Salt and pepper

Equipment
2 saucepans, food processor, ladle, 2-4 jars.

Method
Wash the celery stalks thoroughly and chop up the stalks and the leaves. Add them to a large saucepan. Chop the onion and garlic and add this to the pan with the herbs. Cover the vegetables with water, bring to the boil and simmer, uncovered for about 35 minutes. In a separate pan, heat the stock until just boiling. Drain most of the cooking water from the vegetables, and remove and discard the bay leaves. Pour the stock over the cooked vegetables. Spoon the soup into a food processor and blend until smooth. Return to a clean saucepan. Mix the flour with a little cold water to form a thick liquid. Heat the soup then pour in the flour mix, stirring continuously. Bring back to the boil and cook until thick. It may be necessary to add more water or more flour/water mix to produce the desired consistency. Stir in the grated nutmeg and season to taste. Ladle into hot jars and seal immediately.

Storage
Store jars in the fridge for up to 3 months

Usage
For lunch or as a starter.

Spinach and Lemon Soup

Any spinach that survived the winter will put on a renewed growth now and the quality of the leaves will improve. Spinach is very light and it is surprising just how much you have to harvest to get the desired quantity. In fact, you will pretty much have to fill a carrier bag with leaves to get enough for this recipe!

Ingredients (serves 4)
1 lb (454 g) fresh spinach
Oil or butter for frying
1 medium onion
2 garlic cloves
1 pint (660 ml) chicken stock
Juice of 1 lemon
Salt and pepper

Equipment
1 large saucepan with a lid, food processor, ladle, 2-4 jars.

Method
Wash the spinach and remove any large stalks. Peel and finely chop the onion and garlic. Heat the oil or butter in a frying pan and add the onion and garlic. Fry gently until just beginning to brown. Add the spinach, cover the pan and cook for 5 minutes, stirring occasionally. Pour the chicken stock over the vegetables and cook for a further 10 minutes. Ladle the soup in batches into a blender and process until smooth. Return to the pan; add the lemon juice and season to taste. Either serve hot or ladle into warmed jars and seal immediately.

Storage
Store jars in the fridge for up to 3 months

Usage
For lunch or as a starter.

Citrus Pot Plant Marmalade

Unless you have a heated greenhouse or a sunny conservatory it is not really feasible to grow orange and lemon trees in the UK. However, mini citrus plants make excellent pot plants, assuming you have a suitable bright position for them. The fruit, as well as being very attractive, are edible but not sweet enough to eat raw. It is possible, however, to use the fruit to give drinks a zing or in marmalade. A whole variety of different citrus plants are available including oranges, lemons, limes and limequats (a cross between lime and kumquat). Because the plants and the fruit are both small, this recipe is designed to use just a small quantity of fruit and to produce 2 or 3 jars. It will, however, probably require the addition of a shop bought fruit or two. It is nicest when 3 different fruit are used so if you have, say, a orange and a lemon plant you may like to top it up with a couple of limes. It does, unfortunately, temporarily spoil the appearance of the pot plants but at this time of year they should be flowering and will quickly bear new fruit and, in fact, removing the old fruit does the plant good.

As much of the method for making marmalade is the same as for jam, please read the section of jam making in the Equipment and Techniques chapter before starting if you haven't already done so.

Ingredients (makes 2-3 jars)
1 lb (454 g) fruit
2¼ pt (1225 ml) water
1 lb 11 oz (765 g) sugar

Equipment
Non-metallic bowl, lemon juicer, piece of muslin, food processor, preserving pan, ladle, jam funnel, 2-3 jars.

Method
Wash the fruit and halve them. Squeeze the fruit and put the juice into the bowl. Put the pips etc. into the muslin cloth. Scrape the remaining membranes out of the peels and add those to the muslin too. Shred the peel either with a sharp knife or in a food processor depending on how you like your marmalade and how much time and energy you have! Add the shredded peel to the bowl; tie up the muslin cloth and put that in as well. Pour the water into the bowl, cover and leave it in a cool place at least overnight. This soaking is an essential part of the recipe and the results won't be as good if you omit it.

After the soaking, put the contents of the bowl, including the muslin, into the preserving pan. Slowly bring it to the boil, and simmer gently until the shredded peel is tender. This is likely to take about an hour. Test it by rubbing it between finger and thumb. In the meantime heat the sugar in a cool oven. Remove the muslin and squeeze it to drain any excess liquid back into the pan. Add the sugar to the pan and heat gently and stir until the sugar has completely dissolved. When the sugar is fully dissolved, bring the pan to a full rolling boil and keep it boiling until it reaches its setting point. In the meantime heat the jars in the oven. Whilst the marmalade is still hot ladle it into the hot jars and seal immediately.

Storage
In a cool dark place for up to two years.

Usage
On toast or in cakes. You might like to try it spread over cheese on toast made with light, tangy cheese such as Lancashire. See recipe below as well.

Marmalade Sponge Drops

Ingredients (makes about 8)
2 eggs
2 oz (55g) caster sugar
½ tsp grated citrus fruit zest
Marmalade
1½ oz (45g) dark chocolate

Equipment
Baking sheet, greaseproof paper, saucepan, large mixing bowl, electric whisk, grater, sieve, wire rack.

Method
Preheat oven to 200 °C, 400 °F, gas mark 6. Line a baking sheet with greased paper. Put the eggs and sugar into a large bowl and set it over a pan of simmering water. Whisk until the mixture is pale and thick. Remove from the heat and whisk for a few more minutes then whisk in the citrus fruit zest (choose a fruit suitable for the marmalade you have: e.g. orange zest for orange marmalade). Sift the flour over the mixture and fold in. Put spoonfuls of mixture onto the baking sheet, leaving space between them; one baking sheet should have about 8 spoonfuls on it. Bake for 5 to 8 minutes until golden. Cool for a moment on the baking sheet then remove onto a wire rack to cool completely. Repeat the cooking procedure as necessary until all the mixture is used. Once cool, spread marmalade on the reverse side of every other sponge and sandwich it together with another one. Melt the chocolate either in the microwave or over a pan of hot water then drizzle it over the drops.

Storage
In an airtight container for 3 to 4 days

Usage
As a snack or dessert.

May

In your first year May will be an exciting month in which you can watch your vegetable patch really come alive with plants and you can start looking forward to your first crops. In subsequent years, if you were organised enough in the previous year then May is when you will start to get your first new season crops and the hungry gap will start to be filled.

Every year

Things to do

Brassicas
Brassicas such as **calabrese, broccoli, kale and red cabbage** can be sown in pots or seed trays in May.

Climbing beans
Climbing beans can also be started off in pots this month. They tend to germinate and grow away quite quickly, particularly if warm enough, so don't be in too much of a hurry to sow them as they will become very leggy very quickly. Again, wait until the second or third week in May before sowing these.

Florence fennel
Florence fennel can be sown this month in the same way as you sowed carrots or salad crops (see April).

Herbs
All herb seedlings can be planted out now.

Late peas
Late peas can be sown this month to continue the succession. I don't generally bother with these as I find that they tend to quickly catch up on earlier sown peas and simply crop when the plants are smaller, resulting in lower yields. They also tend to be more prone to getting pea moth maggots in them and, if they do crop slightly later, then they do so at a time when there are plenty of other crops to harvest and they are not necessary.

Potatoes
Finish planting any main crop potatoes you didn't plant last month.

Salad crops
Continue sowing a succession of salad crops directly in the soil.

Sweetcorn
Sow sweetcorn in pots this month. Bare in mind that you can't plant sweetcorn out until all risk of frost as passed but you don't want your plants to get too leggy in the meantime; I would recommend sowing in the second or third week of May. They also benefit from warmth when germinating so put them in a propagator or in a warm room. Once germinated, move them into the cold frame to get enough light but keep the cold frame closed at night to stop it getting too cold. It is said that sweetcorn hate having their roots disturbed, although I have never found this to be a particular problem. However, it may be worth sowing them in individual pots or cells in a seed tray. One trick is to save toilet roll tubes and stand these in a seed tray, fill them with compost and plant one seed per roll. When it comes to planting out you simply bury the tube as well, which then rots away. I have tried this method and found it worked fine, although it was a bit fiddly and the rolls started to go mouldy before they were planted out which was a little unpleasant. You also need a good supply of toilet roll tubes and somewhere to store them until needed.

Tender crops
Check your tender crops and pot them on if necessary. Remember they cannot be planted out until the end of the month. Harden them off in a cold frame if they are big enough but make sure the cold frame does not get too cold at night. If you are really desperate to get things going, or you need cold frame space, or your plants are very leggy, then you might risk planting these crops out by the end of the month, preferably with cloche protection. This is most likely to be possible in the south of the country but it is a risk.

Watercress
This can be pricked out and moved into a larger, suitable container. The container should be very poorly drained or have no drainage holes at all and can now be placed in a shady place outside to grow to maturity.

Things to Expect

Broad beans
Broad beans should flower during May – pretty white and black flowers with a soapy aroma. If your site is very windy the plants may need supporting but generally they support themselves.

Carrots, beetroot and parsnip
Carrot and beetroot should have germinated by now, although parsnips are a little slower and more temperamental. If you don't have any signs of these by the middle of the month then they have either failed to germinate or have been eaten by slugs before you saw them. Don't panic; re-sow as necessary as there is still plenty of time.

Cold frame
Don't forget that slugs and snails can climb, particularly when tempted by all the lush vegetation of your tender crops. You may need slug protection measures in and around your cold frame so that you don't lose your plants before you have even planted them out.

Onions and shallots
These should have obvious green leaves by now. If not then chances are that bulb has failed and will never grow.

Peas and mangetout
These should germinate around the beginning of the month, grow away quickly (get in support now if you didn't do it when you sowed them!) and should be flowering by the end of the month.

Potatoes
All potato varieties should emerge during May.

Soil
If May is very dry and you have heavy clay soil then it may well set like concrete now which can make weeding and sowing difficult. Water the soil if necessary, allow a few minutes for the water to drain through then try working on it.

Weeds
As the weather warms up and while it is still damp, weeds will really take off. It is important to try to keep on top of them or weeds will out-compete tiny seedlings for light and water.

Things to harvest
Watercress

Watercress Soup

Ingredients (serves 2)
Oil (for frying)
1 small onion
1 small to medium potato (4 oz, 110 g)
4 oz watercress
1 pint (600 ml) stock (chicken or vegetable)
Lime juice
Salt and pepper

Equipment
Large saucepan, spatula, food processor/blender, 2 clean jars with "safety" buttons.

Method
Strip the leaves from the watercress and chop the stalks. Finely chop the onions and peel and dice the potato. Heat the oil in the bottom of a large saucepan and fry the onions over a gentle heat until softened. Add the potatoes and fry for 2 to 3 minutes, then cover and continue to cook for 5 minutes, stirring occasionally. Add the stock to the saucepan, stir in the stalks and bring back to the boil. Simmer gently for 10 minutes until the potatoes are tender or mushy. Add the watercress leaves and simmer for a further 2 minutes. Remove from the heat and blend the soup in a food processor until smooth. Return the soup to a clean saucepan and heat. Season to taste with salt and pepper and lime juice then serve, or pour into warmed jars and seal.

Storage
Once the soup has cooled the safety button should have become depressed again. If it has, then it can be stored for a few months, if not then use within 3 days.

Usage
This makes attractive green soup with a gentle flavour. It can be used as a light snack with bread or as a starter.

Subsequent years

Things to expect

Asparagus

Asparagus beetle will emerge this month. This is a small, black beetle with distinctive orange spots on its back. They are most harmful to asparagus during their first and second years, after which time the plants are so well established that they don't do much harm. They are very quick movers so squashing them can be a challenge and you may have to resort to spraying.

Bolting

Leeks will bolt during May and become completely inedible. Mind you, if left they produce flower stalks 5 or 6 feet tall and flowers the size of your fist or head! They are quite spectacular and the insects, including bees, absolutely love them. Any **carrots, beetroot, parsnips and celery** will also bolt during this month. Parsnips in particular will self-seed all over the place if you let them. Unfortunately, self-sown parsnips tend to be more like wild parsnips with a long, thin woody root that is not particularly edible and quite difficult to remove.

Fruit

Currants, cherries, plums, peaches, strawberries and apples will start to form fruit during May, although if it is your first year then your yield may be low (or non-existent).

Things to harvest
Asparagus
Bolted vegetables (see recipe below)
Japanese onions
Spring onions

In the kitchen

Bolted Vegetable Stock

This is a good use for vegetables that are otherwise too tough to eat. Be aware that the centre of the bolted vegetables might be so tough that you can't chop them with a knife. Try snapping them or using them whole.

Ingredients
6 - 12 bolted leeks (depending on size)
12 or so medium bolted carrots
3 - 4 bolted celery sticks
4 garlic cloves

2 sprigs of rosemary
4 sprigs of sage
4 bay leaves
3 pints (1700g) water
Salt and pepper

Equipment
Knife, large saucepan (e.g. preserving pan or casserole), sieve, funnel, 3 clean jars (ideally with a "safety button")

Method
Wash the leeks, top and tail and coarsely chop. Wash the carrots and break into pieces. Top and tail the celery and cut into pieces. Add all the vegetables to the saucepan, along with either fresh or dried herbs and garlic. Season with salt and pepper. Add a whole kettle full of boiling water, bring back to the boil and simmer for 15-20 minutes. Sieve over a funnel into warmed jars or bottles and seal immediately.

Storage
Once the stock has cooled the safety button should have become depressed again. If it has, then the stock can be stored for a few months, if not then use within 3 days. Do not be surprised if the colour of the stock changes from a green to a brown colour as it matures.

Usage
In any recipe requiring stock such as soups, casseroles, bakes and hotpots (see other recipes in this book).

Herb Mustard

These can be made at any time of year when you have an ample supply of herbs. I have suggested making them in May because the foliage tends to be young and fresh and by June the herbs are concentrating of producing flowers, resulting in a lack of vigour in the leaves. The end of the summer is another good time to make herb mustard and is a good way to preserve the flavour of herbs for use over winter.

Ingredients
½ oz (15 g) fresh herbs (e.g. sage, thyme or rosemary)
2 oz (50 g) plain flour
2¾ oz (75 g) mustard powder
1 oz (25 g) caster sugar

1 tbsp salt
3½ fl oz (100 ml) white wine vinegar

Equipment
Knife, sieve, bowl, 3 × 75ml mustard jars

Method
Strip the herbs from their stalks and finely chop the leaves. Sift the flour and mustard powder into a bowl. Add the caster sugar and salt and mix well. Add the herbs and vinegar and stir until it forms a paste. Spoon the mustard into clean jars and seal.

Storage
Keep in a cool, dark place for a least a week before using to allow the flavours to develop. Refrigerate once opened but it can be used for months even after opening.

Usage
The mustard can be used straight from the jar as a table condiment but seems to develop a far superior flavour when used in cooking (see recipe ideas below).

Pork Chops with Sage Mustard

Ingredients
2 pork chops
2 small shallots or one medium onion
1 dessert spoon of sage mustard
Salt and pepper

Equipment
Sharp knife, butter knife

Method
Cover grill pan with foil. Slice the onion or shallots into rings and place it on the foil in a single layer. Season one side of the chop with salt and freshly ground pepper. Smear the mustard over this side of the chop (being careful not to contaminate the mustard in the jar with raw meat!). Place the chop mustard side down on top of shallots so that no shallots are showing. Season the reverse side of chop with salt and pepper. Grill the chop, turning occasionally. Shortly before the chop is completely cooked uncover the shallots and allow them to brown slightly. Serve immediately with the shallots on top of the chop.

As the basis of a meal for two with suitable accompaniment.
Variations
Alternatively substitute the pork chops for lamb chops and the sage mustard for rosemary or thyme mustard.

Roast Beef with Rosemary Mustard

Ingredients
1 joint of beef (of your choosing)
1 tbsp rosemary mustard
Salt and pepper

Equipment
Butter knife

Method
Prepare the joint as normal. Season the exposed meat (not fat) of the joint with salt and pepper then smear with mustard (being careful not to contaminate the mustard in the jar with raw meat!). Roast the joint in the normal manner and use the juices to make gravy.

Usage
As the basis of a roast dinner.

Variations
Rosemary or thyme mustard can be used to prepare lamb in the same way. Lamb is even more delicious if you coarsely chop a clove of garlic and push pieces into cuts made in the meat before covering in mustard. Sage mustard can be used to prepare pork joints.

Asparagus Stem Soup

There are numerous recipes for asparagus soup, all suggesting the use of the tender tips. However, it seems such as waste of precious tips to put them in soup rather than to merely steam them and serve them simply in a way where the delicate flavour can be appreciated. In this recipe, the tougher, inedible parts of the stem are used, allowing the flavour of asparagus to prevail whilst making good use of something that would otherwise be thrown away.

Ingredients

For every 1 lb (450g) asparagus stems use:

¾ oz (20 g) butter
2 small onions (or shallots)
¾ oz (20 g) flour
10 fl oz (285 ml) chicken stock
1 bay leaf
Water
Salt and pepper

NB: 1½ lb (700g) asparagus makes approximately 2 servings

Equipment

Large saucepan, knife, spatula, coarse sieve, ladle, food processor/blender, bowl, funnel, 1-2 clean jars (ideally with a "safety button")

Method

Chop the stems into pieces and cook for about 20 minutes then set aside. If necessary the stems can be frozen at this point and used at a later date or accumulated until you have enough. Chop the onions finely. Melt the butter in the bottom of the saucepan and gently fry the onions until soft. Gradually add flour, stirring constantly so that it does not stick to the bottom. Pour in the chicken stock and bring the mixture to the boil whist stirring. Add the drained asparagus and bay leaf. Simmer for about 25 to 30 minutes until the asparagus has softened – add additional water during simmering if necessary to retain a thick soup consistency. Ladle the soup into a blender in batches and blend briefly. Do not expect to blend it until smooth, as the woody stems are very fibrous. Pour into a coarse sieve over a bowl and force it through until you have liquid in the bowl and dry pulpy fibres in the sieve. Return the liquid to the saucepan, bring it to the boil and season if necessary. Either serve it hot or pour it into hot jars and seal immediately.

Storage

Once the soup has cooled the safety button should have become depressed again. If it has, then the soup can be stored for several months, if not then use within 3 days.

Usage

Serve with bread for a light meal, snack or starter.

Duck in Oyster Sauce with Spring and Japanese Onions

Although you can buy duck legs (or even breasts) for this recipe, it is an ideal way of using up leg meat from a whole roast duck. Roast the duck (stuffed with sage and onion) and serve the breast up as one delicious meal then make this recipe the next day with the cold leg meat.

Ingredients
Oil (for frying)
4 - 5 spring onions
2 Japanese onions (or 2 medium onions from storage)
1 inch (2.5 cm) piece of root ginger (skin removed)
Freshly ground black pepper
Cooked duck meat (e.g. 2 legs)
One bottle of oyster sauce
6½ oz (180) g brown rice (or substitute with 7oz (200g) white rice if preferred)

Equipment
Knife, large frying pan, saucepan, spatula

Method
Chop the spring onions into 2 or 3 pieces then slice lengthways into thin strips. Coarsely chop the Japanese onions. Slice the root ginger into broad pieces. In the meantime remove the cooked meat from the bone. When the rice has about 8 minutes left to cook, heat the oil in the frying pan. Add the meat, onions, ginger and pepper and stir-fry for 5 to 7 minutes until the meat is hot through and onions are soft but not brown. Add the jar of oyster sauce and heat through. Serve immediately with the rice.

Usage
As a meal for 2.

June

All being well, you will have your first glut of crops this month. I always think of June as the strawberry and mangetout month as these are the first things to be ready to pick and once they are in full swing I have to harvest them every 2 days just to keep up with them! It is a busy month both on the plot and in the kitchen. Although there is still lots to do on the plot, you will be rewarded with fresh, tasty fruit and vegetables and you'll decide that the effort is worthwhile.

Every Year

Things to do

Broccoli, Calabrese and Cabbage
These can be planted out this month. If they have become leggy then bury a good deal of the leggy stem when you plant them. Brassicas need firm soil to stop them from falling over once they are bigger. They also benefit from lime unless your soil is naturally very alkaline, which is unlikely. They will need protecting from pigeons too. Pigeons love brassica leaves and strip even mature plants to bare stems in a day. Either put individual bottle cloches over each plant at this stage or net all of them. It is best to protect them from slugs too. If you want broccoli and kale to harvest from February onwards then sow seeds for these this month, either in trays or directly in the ground.

Climbing beans
Before planting out your climbing beans you need to dig out a trench and infill it with something to retain moisture such as well-rotted manure, grass cuttings or strips of newspaper. You will then need to erect some 6 or 7 feet canes in a good solid shape to give the plants something to grow up. Each plant needs its own pole, string or bit of netting to grow up. It is also possible to sow beans directly in the soil at this time of year. Remember slug protection.

Dwarf Beans
Dwarf beans can be sown directly in the soil this month. They crop slightly sooner than climbing beans because they concentrate less on foliage and height but the yield is generally lower.

Leeks
Leeks can be planted this month. The method for planting leeks seems bizarrely cruel but they seem to like it. Cut off about a third of the seedling's roots and leaves, bore a hole in the soil with a dipper

that is slightly larger than the seedling and drop it into it. Without filling in the hole with soil, water in the leek, allowing the water to take some soil with it.

Potatoes
Main crop potatoes should be earthed up. To do this, pull soil up around the plant. Don't worry about putting too much soil on the plant – even a completely buried plant will quickly re-emerge. New tubers should form on the buried stems, thus increasing your yield. Remove fleece from first early potatoes if you have not already done so.

Soil
The soil can become very dry in June so monitor crops for water requirements. Young crops and the tender crops need most attention. Also keep weeds in check.

Sweetcorn
Sweetcorn need to be planted in a box shape because they are wind pollinated plants. Fairly close planting (approximately 8 to 12 inches between plants) in a square enables good pollination. Mini sweetcorn does not need to be pollinated so can be grown in rows.

Tender crops
All your tender crops can be planted out this month. These include tomatoes, peppers, aubergines, cape gooseberries, basil, pumpkins, cucumbers, gherkins, melons, courgettes, celery and lablab beans. It is a good idea to erect 4 to 6 feet stakes next to every tomato plant unless it is a bush or trailing variety. It may look unlikely when you plant them but in a month or two's time they will be that tall and needing support – better to put them in now rather than force them through the root ball later. Most tomatoes will be grown as cordons rather than bushes. To do this, you need to regularly tie the central stem to the stake, and remove any side-shoots as they appear.

Temperamental crops such as peppers, aubergines and melons do better if you dig out a deep hole and infill it with rotted manure first before planting the plants on top. The heat from the manure as it decomposes helps to keep the plant warm and when the plants' roots get bigger they will have a good supply of nutrients to use to grow fruit. A fleece tunnel over these plants at this time also helps to keep them warm (without stopping water reaching them) and gets them off to a very good start, hopefully allowing enough time for fruit formation and ripening before the frosts in October.

Things to expect

Broccoli, Calabrese and Cabbage

Once outside brassicas should quickly take on a much more sturdy appearance and put on more leaf. You may also notice cabbage white butterflies taking an interest in them and it is worth checking for small clutches of eggs on the underside of the leaves. These will develop into hundreds of caterpillars by August so dispatching them now may be more convenient, if a little sad for the butterfly.

Broad beans
Blackfly will appear on broad beans during June. It is said that pinching out the growing tip helps to control blackfly on broad beans but in my experience the blackfly end up all over the plant, being helped and protected by their own private army of ants. If you don't mind using chemicals then you can spray the blackfly, although it is best to do this last thing in the evening so you limit poisoning beneficial insects such as ladybirds and bees that are attracted to the flowers. Alternatively, you could try spraying with soapy water or blasting them with a strong hosepipe. This doesn't kill anything, including the blackfly, but it does knock quite a lot off and can limit the damage they do. It is also said that planting garlic or savory between the rows of broad beans can limit blackfly infestation. I have tried both and found the garlic didn't grow well because the bean plants overshadowed it so had limited affect. Savory is a perennial so it is not convenient to plant it between rows of an annual, particularly when observing a crop rotation scheme.

Courgettes and cucumbers
Large, yellow flowers should appear on these this month. Cucumbers will happily ramble across the ground but you might find it more convenient to grow them up a stake, particularly as this helps to keep the fruit clean and unblemished. Courgettes grow outwards and don't need to be staked.

Peas and mangetout
Not only should they be flowering but pods should also be forming by now.

Tomatoes
These will grow rapidly and need to be checked for side-shoots and the need for extra ties at least once a week. Flowers will appear and fruit will begin to form during June.

Things to harvest
Beetroot and carrot thinnings
Broad beans
Cherries
Courgettes
Gooseberries (green)
Mangetout
New potatoes
Peas
Red currants
Strawberries
Tayberries
Watercress

Harvesting techniques

Beetroot
Wait until the beets are ping-pong ball size before thinning so that the thinnings can be eaten or pickled as whole baby beets (see January for recipe). Simply twist off the foliage. Some people recommend eating the foliage as a spinach type vegetable but at this time of year you may not need any extra vegetables so the tops can be composted.

Broad beans
Although the pods will quickly become large, it takes a while for the beans inside to develop so squeeze the pods to feel for beans inside. Some people like to harvest a few pods whilst still empty and cook them and eat them like runner beans. Whenever you harvest the pods, pull them downward to rip them off the plant. Beans are best when they are still small, with their green tags still attached to the inside of the pod. Once the tags become yellow, drop off and reveal a black scar on the bean then you know the bean will be tough.

Carrots
Wait until the carrots are about as thick as a pencil before thinning them out. Thinning is essential to allow the remaining plants to have the space to develop into thick roots but you may as well wait until the thinnings are big enough to eat before doing this. If the soil is very dry, water it first and allow it to sink in then it should be possible to pull the carrots up without snapping off their foliage. Remove all carrot debris from the site, as the smell will attract the carrot root fly. Twist off the foliage and add it to the compost bin before taking the thinnings to the kitchen to help prevent dehydration of the root.

Cherries

You will probably have a battle on your hands to pick cherries before the birds get to them. One method of deterring them is to net the cherry tree if it is small enough. However, you may find some determined birds find their way inside the netting but then cannot find their way out again and you have the unpleasant task of having to free a trapped bird, which is distressing all round. An alternative is to pick the cherries just as they are turning red and leave them on your windowsill for a few days to ripen fully. It is particularly useful if you intend to use the cherries in recipes rather than just eating them because slightly under ripe cherries generally cook better.

Courgettes

Beware that courgette plant stems and the underside of the leaves can be surprisingly spiky. When harvesting the fruit try to avoid catching your hands and arms or the fruit on the spikes as the skin on all of them can be damaged. Rotate the fruit and it should twist off, or alternatively cut the stem with a knife.

Mangetout

You may as well start harvesting them when they are still a bit on the small side. These first small, tender pods are delicious and you will soon have a glut anyway. Expect to have to harvest every other day to keep on top of production and each time harvest all the pods to encourage new growth. If any pod is missed and swells to maturity the plant will stop flowering and the harvest will stop so be careful to search them out. By the second week of cropping you will have more than you can eat but they can be stored in a closed plastic bag in the fridge for 2 to 3 weeks and still be in better condition than those you get in a supermarket!

New potatoes

It is usually worth scraping back the soil first to find the tubers. If they are ready, use a fork to gently lift the plant. Push the fork into the ground further away from the plant than you expect the tubers to be because it is all too easy to stick a fork tine right through the middle of an otherwise beautiful spud. Remove one plant at a time, composting the foliage, and thoroughly checking the soil for missed potatoes. Any potatoes you miss now will pop up again next year, right in the middle of another crop. You will miss some potatoes no matter how thorough you are!

Peas
The key to harvesting peas is not to underestimate how many pods you will need. Once they are shelled there is a lot less pea than you imagined. I would say you need 20 to 30 pods per portion. Wait until the pods are swollen before harvesting them but don't wait until the pod skin becomes leathery. Pick all that are ready to encourage a new crop. When shelling, don't be too shocked to find the occasional pea moth maggot, particularly during July.

Strawberries
At this time of year everything is hungry so your first ripe strawberries will be prone to slug and/or bird attack. You could try placing each bunch of unripe fruit into a plastic bottle with its bottom cut off. Not only does this speed up ripening but it keeps the fruit clean and can help prevent nibbles. Alternatively, you can console yourself with the knowledge that by the second week of harvest the damage will be lessened. It is worth harvesting damaged (but not mouldy) fruit (within reason) as they can be successfully used in recipes even if you don't fancy eating them.

Cooking tips

Beetroot
Wash the roots but don't cut into them in any way or they will bleed. Boil some water in a kettle. Sort the beets into roots of approximately equal sizes and boil them in separate batches. Ping-pong ball sized roots need about half an hour, golf ball size need about 40 minutes, tennis ball size need 50 to 60 minutes. Drain and leave to cool. Store in a sealed plastic food bag for up to 5 days in the fridge. To serve, rub off the skin between your fingers, top and tail and cut as required.

Broad beans
If the beans are young and tender then boil in unsalted water (salt makes the skins tough) for 3 to 5 minutes depending on size. For added flavour, include a couple of sprigs of savory in the water whilst boiling. Drain and serve immediately – including the savory, then season if necessary. Older beans will need longer boiling times and may also need their skins removing after cooking if very tough.

Carrots
Thinned carrots are too small to peel but they should be cleaned and can be scraped with a fingernail. They can be eaten whole or in halves depending on their size. Boil in lightly salted water for about 5 minutes.

Courgettes

The simplest way to cook courgettes is to cut them into rounds, season then stir-fry – with chopped garlic and ginger if you like – for about 3 to 5 minutes until just beginning to brown on either side.

Mangetout

Top and tail each pod using your fingernails or by snapping off. Any stringiness should come away at this point too. Bring to the boil in lightly salted water and simmer for 3 minutes, drain and serve immediately. Alternatively, steam for 3 minutes.

New potatoes

Wash and scrape (if necessary). If small enough leave the potato whole or cut it if necessary. It is best to avoid cooking a combination of uncut and cut spuds at the same time because the cut ones cook quicker than uncut. Bring the potatoes to the boil in lightly salted water and simmer for 5 to 15 minutes depending on the variety and size. Use a fork to check they are soft. Cooking your first batch of potatoes will be a bit of guesswork as every variety varies considerably in its cooking time. When soft but still firm enough not to fall to pieces, drain and serve. They can be served on their own, with butter and chopped mint, with olive oil and black pepper, with grated cheese or any number of other possibilities.

Peas

Shell the peas and compost the pods. Bring the peas to the boil in unsalted water (salt makes the skins tough). Simmer for 3 minutes, drain and serve immediately and season if necessary. For added flavour, include a sprig of mint in the water a minute or two before ready and sprinkle chopped mint over the portion to serve.

Preserving Tips

Freezing

Of all the vegetables ready in June I would only recommend freezing **broad bean and peas**. **Mangetout** really don't stand freezing well although they can be used at a pinch in stir-fries. Both broad beans and peas, however, stand the freezing process and it is a good way to deal with any glut now rather than allowing the pods to stand on the plant too long and over mature. Before freezing, blanch and dry (see Equipment and Techniques chapter). When freezing broad beans, it is nice to include some savory too.

Strawberries can be frozen successfully without blanching for use later in jams etc. It can be useful to freeze fruit as it ripens and accumulate it in the freezer until you have a large enough batch for jam making. Do not freeze fruit if you are intending to use it in ice cream because it would have to be refrozen (without cooking) once in the ice cream which increases the risk of food poisoning. The fruit is mushy once thawed so is not suited for eating in the same way as fresh fruit.

Pickling

The conventional way to preserve **beetroot** is to pickle it. See January for a recipe for pickled whole beets. If the beetroot it larger, simply cut into slices or chucks before preserving in the same way.

In the Kitchen

It is very easy to get a glut of strawberries even from only a few plants. Of course, they are delicious served with sugar and cream or yoghurt. However, there are only so many strawberries you can eat each day and only so many days in a row you can eat them. Therefore, it is useful to be able to preserve them and to enjoy their taste even in the murkiness of winter. However, there is also a limit to the amount of strawberry jam you can tolerate! Below I have given a number of recipes that use strawberries. Some simply give an alternative use for fresh strawberries whilst most provide a way of preserving them. As with all things, I think variety is key so I have provided lots of ideas for you to try.

Strawberry Jam

Please read the section on jam making in the Equipment and Techniques chapter before starting this recipe.

Words of caution

Despite how common and familiar strawberry jam is, it is one of the most difficult jams to make successfully. Strawberries are a low pectin fruit, which is why lemons are needed. To remove as much pectin as possible, it is important to heat the strawberries gently and no water should be added. It is also important to use fresh lemons rather than bottled juice and to be generous with it. Be very thorough to ensure that all the sugar is dissolved before bringing to a vigorous boil because any undissolved sugar will burn and cause your jam to darken and take on the taste of burnt sugar. Check thoroughly that the setting point is reached too to avoid runny jam.

Ingredients (makes 5 to 6 jars)
3 lb (1400 g) strawberries
2 lb 10 oz (1200 g) sugar
2 large lemons providing about 3½ fl oz (100 ml) of juice

NB: Every pound of strawberries requires 14 oz (400g) sugar and 2 tb sp (30 ml) of lemon juice.

Equipment
Preserving pan, wooden spoon, large ovenproof dish, lemon juicer, ladle, jam funnel, 5 to 6 clean jars.

Method
For this recipe any strawberries, whether whole, damaged, squashed, fresh or frozen can be used. Pick the strawberries over, removing any green stalks but don't bother to chop them up. Place the strawberries in the preserving pan and heat very gently, stirring continuously with a wooden spoon until they begin to break up. Simmer for 20 minutes until the fruit is soft. In the meantime, juice the lemons, weigh out the sugar and preheat an oven to 100 °C, 200 °F; gas mark ¼. Place the sugar in an ovenproof dish and warm in the oven. Once the fruit is soft, add the sugar to the pan and stir in, over a low heat until all the sugar is completely dissolved. Add the lemon juice and boil vigorously until the setting point is reached. Pour into warmed jars and seal immediately.

Storage
Store in a cool dark place for up to two years.

Usage
On bread and toast, in cakes and tarts, in porridge and in flapjacks (see below)

Strawberry and Cherry Flapjacks

Ingredients (makes 12)
4¾ oz (135 g) margarine
5¼ oz (150 g) strawberry jam
8 oz (225 g) oats
Pinch of salt

¾ oz (20 g) sunflower seeds
1¾ oz (50 g) glacé cherries (chopped)

Equipment
9-inch (23-cm) square cake tin, large saucepan, wooden spoon.

Method
Preheat oven to 190 °C, 375 °F, gas mark 5. Line and grease the cake tin. In a large saucepan, gently melt together the margarine and the jam. Remove from the heat and add the oats, salt, seeds and cherries. Stir well until fully combined. Spoon the mixture into the cake tin and press down well with wetted fingers. Bake for 15 to 20 minutes until golden brown. Mark out to 12 pieces then allow to cool completely in the tin.

Storage
Store in an airtight container for up to a week.

Usage
As a filling, nutritious snack.

Strawberry Crumble Muffins

Ingredients (makes 12)
For muffins:
7¼ oz (200 g) self-raising flour
5 oz (140 g) plain flour
3¾ oz (105 g) dark brown sugar
5 oz (140 g) small fresh or frozen strawberries (cut into pieces if necessary)
2 eggs
8 fl oz (225 ml) milk
4 oz (110 g) butter

For topping:
1¾ oz (50 g) plain flour
1 oz (25 g) butter
2 tb sp dark brown sugar

Equipment
2 × bowls, sieve, fork, muffin tin, muffin cases, wire rack, skewer.

Method
Preheat oven to 210 °C, 410 °F, gas mark 6½. Sift the flours into a bowl and stir in the sugar and strawberries. Make a well in the centre. Whisk the eggs and milk together and pour into the well. Melt the butter and pour in as well. Stir the mixture with a fork until just combined – do not over mix. Place 12 muffin cases in a muffin tin and spoon the mixture evenly between them so that each case is about three-quarters full. In a small bowl, rub together the flour, butter and sugar for the topping until crumbly. Sprinkle this on top of each muffin and press on gently. Cook for about 20 minutes until a skewer comes out clean. Cool in the tin for 5 minutes before transferring onto a wire rack.

Storage
Keep in an airtight container for up to a week.

Usage
Serve whilst still warm, eat cold or reheat in the microwave. Can be served on their own, with custard, cream or ice cream.

Strawberry and Marshmallow Ice cream

Here's one for the kids and a good use of damaged strawberries too!

Ingredients
1½ lb (700 g) strawberries
5 oz (140 g) icing sugar
1½ tsp lemon juice
8 oz (225 g) marshmallows
7½ fl oz (210 ml) milk
½ pint (300 ml) double cream

Equipment
Puree equipment (see Equipment and Techniques chapter), bowl, microwavable bowl, whisk, and plastic containers (see Equipment and Techniques chapter).

Method
Puree the strawberries so that you are left with a seedless liquid. Add the sugar and lemon juice and stir until the sugar is dissolved. Put half the marshmallows and the milk into a suitable bowl and heat in the microwave for 2 minutes to melt them. Stir this mixture, add the cream and whisk lightly so that it thickens slightly. Combine with the

strawberry puree, mixing until the mixture is evenly pink. Add the remaining marshmallows, pour into suitable containers and place in the freezer for 3 hours. Remove from the freezer and beat the ice cream to introduce air, to break any ice crystals and to distribute the marshmallows throughout the ice cream.

Storage
Store in the freezer for up to a year.

Usage
Remove container from the freezer about twenty minutes or half an hour before you wish to serve it to soften it enough to serve it easily.

Strawberry Ice cream

This is a more "grown-up" version of ice cream!

Ingredients
1 lb (450 g) strawberries
3 oz (85 g) icing sugar
1 tsp lemon juice
½ pint (300 ml) double cream
Semi-skimmed milk
2 tsp vanilla extract

Equipment
Pureeing equipment (see Equipment and Techniques chapter), bowl, whisk, and plastic containers (see Equipment and Techniques chapter).

Method
Puree the strawberries so that you are left with a seedless liquid. Add the sugar and lemon juice and stir until the sugar is dissolved. Measure this mixture then make up the cream to the same quantity with milk. Add the vanilla extract and whip until it just begins to thicken. Combine the cream and the puree until evenly pink. Pour into suitable containers and place in the freezer for 3 hours. Remove from the freezer and beat then return to the freezer.

Storage
Store in the freezer for up to a year.

Usage

Remove from the freezer 20 minutes to half an hour before you wish to serve it to soften it enough to serve it easily. The mixture can also be used to make strawberry ice cream lollies by being poured into lolly moulds instead of plastic contains. These can be served straight from the freezer. This ice cream is also used in the "Posh Preserved Strawberry Dessert" recipe below.

Strawberry and Orange Conserve

Ingredients (makes about 1 jar)
12 oz (340 g) best quality, whole strawberries, hulled.
Grated rind and juice of 1 small orange
1 tb sp lemon juice
8 oz (225 g) granulated or caster sugar
1 tb sp Cointreau

Equipment
Non-metallic bowl, preserving pan (or large saucepan), 1 clean jar.

Method
Place all the strawberries, rind and orange and lemon juice in a bowl. Sprinkle over the sugar and gently toss the fruit to thoroughly coat. Place in the refrigerator for 2 days. Tip the fruit into a preserving pan and bring slowly to the boil. Boil for 5 to 7 minutes, stirring frequently to prevent sticking but gently so not to break up fruit. Remove from the heat and pour in the Cointreau. Transfer to a warmed jar and seal immediately.

Storage
Store in a cool, dark place for up to a year.

Usage
Can be used as an attractive and tasty accompaniment to suitable desserts and ice cream. Is used in the "Posh Preserved Strawberry Dessert" recipe below.

Posh Preserved Strawberry Dessert

Ingredients (serves 6)
1 packet of 6 dark chocolate cases
6 tb sp strawberry and orange conserve

6 scoops of strawberry ice cream
Fresh mint leaves (to garnish)

Equipment
6 serving dishes, tablespoon, ice cream scoop.

Method
Take the strawberry ice cream out of the freezer 20-30 minutes before required. Into each dark chocolate case, place a tablespoon of strawberry and orange conserve. Top each case with a scoop of strawberry ice cream and garnish with a sprig of mint if desired. Serve immediately.

Usage
Serves 6 people as a light, sophisticated dessert at the end of a dinner party. It is particularly appealing if served later in the year when strawberries are no longer in season to give you a reminder of the taste of summer.

Strawberry and Gooseberry Jam

This is a good recipe for the end of June when the strawberry crop is winding down and the gooseberries are just becoming ripe. The strawberries dominate the overall taste but the gooseberries are high in pectin and it makes a much firmer jam with a more successful setting rate than normal strawberry jam. If you haven't already done so, please read the jam making section of the Equipment and Techniques chapter first.

Ingredients (makes 4-5 jars)
1 lb 5 oz (600 g) gooseberries
1 lb 5 oz (600 g) strawberries (fresh or frozen)
8 fl oz (225 ml) water
2 lb 10 oz (740 g) sugar

Equipment
Preserving pan, knife, wooden spoon, ovenproof dish, ladle, jam funnel, 4 to 5 jars.

Method
Top and tail the gooseberries and place in the preserving pan. If using frozen strawberries add these now, but if using fresh strawberries wait until the gooseberries are beginning to soften before adding. Add the

water to the pan and bring slowly to the boil. Simmer for about 20 minutes until the fruit is soft and pulpy. In the meantime, heat the sugar in an oven set to 100 °C, 200 °F; gas mark ¼. Once the fruit is pulpy, add the sugar and stir constantly until it has fully dissolved. Bring to the boil and boil for about 10 minutes until the setting point is reached. Check for setting then ladle into warmed jars and seal immediately.

Storage
Store in a cool, dark place for up to 2 years.

Usage
As for strawberry jam.

Gooseberry Chutney

Ingredients (makes about 2 jars)
2½ lb (1100 g) just ripe green gooseberries
½ pint (250 ml) white wine vinegar
4 oz (115 g) raisins
4 oz (115 g) sultanas
1 large onion
1 lb (455 g) soft dark brown sugar
½ tsp turmeric
2 tsp freshly ground black pepper
1 tsp mixed spice
1 tsp cinnamon

Equipment
Preserving pan, wooden spoon, knife, ladle, jam funnel, 2 clean jars

Method
Wash and top and tail the gooseberries. Finely chop the onion. Place the gooseberries in the preserving pan and add the vinegar. Bring to the boil and simmer for 10 to 20 minutes until the fruit is soft and pulpy. Add all the other ingredients and bring slowly back to the boil, stirring continuously so that the sugar dissolves. Simmer for 1 to 2 hours until it is thick. Test for thickness (as described in Equipment and Techniques chapter). Ladle into hot jars and seal immediately.

Storage
Store for 2 to 3 months before use to allow flavours to develop and mature then use within a year.

Usage
Goes well with cheese or smoked fish. Can be used in smoked salmon sandwiches.

Cherry and Ginger Sauce

Ingredients (makes about 2 bottles)
12 oz (340 g) fresh cherries
1 oz (25 g) caster sugar
3 tbsp water
2 fl oz (55 ml) red wine vinegar
¼ pt (100 ml) port
1 tbsp fresh lemon juice
¼ tsp lemon zest
½ pt (300 ml) stock (chicken or duck)
2 inch (5 cm) piece of root ginger (cut in half)
1½ tsp cornflour
Salt and freshly ground black pepper

Equipment
Non-stick pan with lid, wooden spoon, grater, knife, food processor, ladle, funnel, 2 clean bottles (approximately 5 fl oz; 150 ml)

Method
Pick over the cherries and rinse them under cold running water then drain. Cut the cherries in half and remove the stone. Set aside. Combine the sugar and water in a small, non-stick saucepan. Cover and heat strongly for 2 minutes. Uncover the pan, reduce the heat and cook until the sugar caramelises. This should take about 6 to 8 minutes and you need to keep a close eye on it as it may suddenly burn. Remove the pan from the heat and add the vinegar. Stand back as you do this as it will hiss and let off vinegar vapours. Return the mixture to a low heat and stir until the caramel has completely dissolved in the vinegar. Stir in the port, lemon juice and zest and bring to the boil. Add the stock and the ginger and cook for 5 minutes. Add the cherries and simmer gently for about 15 minutes until the cherries are soft. At the same time, heat 2 bottle in an oven at 100 °C, 200 °F, gas mark ¼. Remove and discard half the ginger. Mix the cornflour with a little cold water then add it to the sauce and boil and stir until the sauce thickens. Add salt and pepper to taste. Pour the sauce into a blender and liquidise. Pour the hot sauce into the preheated bottles and seal immediately.

Storage
Stores for up to a year in sealed bottles. Refrigerate and use within 3 days once opened. Alternatively, freeze any unused sauce.

Usage
This is an excellent accompaniment to game, particularly duck, either as a pour on sauce or as a dipping sauce. Heat before serving either in the microwave or on the hob.

Cherry and Red Currant Jam

This is a good recipe for combining small quantities of two fruits. Cherries are low in pectin and it is difficult to make a cherry jam set. However, red currants are very high in pectin so combining the two makes a jam that sets very well. The two flavours are also frequently used to accompany game meats so this jam can be used with meat as well as a conventional jam. If you haven't already done so, please read the jam making section of the Equipment and Techniques chapter first.

Ingredients (makes 1-2 jars)
8 oz (225g) cherries
8 oz (225g) red currants
8 oz (225g) sugar
4 tbsp water

Equipment
Preserving pan, knife, wooden spoon, ovenproof dish, ladle, jam funnel, 1 to 2 jars.

Method
Cut the cherries in half and remove the stones then place in the preserving pan. Strip the red currants from their stalks and add to the pan. Add the water to the pan and bring slowly to the boil. Simmer for about 10-15 minutes until the fruit is soft and pulpy. In the meantime, heat the sugar in an oven set to 100 °C, 200 °F; gas mark ¼. Once the fruit is pulpy, add the sugar and stir constantly until it has fully dissolved. Bring to the boil and boil for about 5 minutes until the setting point is reached. Check for setting then ladle into warmed jars and seal immediately.

Storage
Store in a cool, dark place for up to 2 years.

Usage

As for any jam. Can also be used as an accompaniment to game meat (such as duck), or as the basis of a sweet sauce to serve with game.

Cherry Pie

Ingredients (makes 1)

For the filling:
6 oz (170 g) dessert cherries
4 fl oz (115 ml) water
4 oz (115 g) sugar
2 tbsp cornflour
3 tsp lemon juice

For the pastry:
4 oz (115 g) plain flour
4 oz (115 g) wholemeal flour (alternatively, use a total of 8 oz, 230 g plain flour)
4 oz (115 g) margarine
2 oz (55 g) caster sugar
Water
A little egg or milk to glaze

Equipment

Knife, saucepan, wooden spoon, bowl, sieve, rolling pin, pie dish.

Method

Cut the cherries in half and remove the stones then place in a saucepan with the water. Bring the cherries to the boil then simmer for 10 minutes. Remove from the heat whilst you add the sugar and the lemon juice. Mix the cornflour with a little cold water then pour it into the cherry mix. Return the mix to the heat and stir as you bring it back to the boil. Continue to stir until the filling is thick.

Preheat the oven to 180 °C, 350 °F, gas mark 3.

To make the pastry: sieve the flours into a bowl, including any bran left in the sieve. Add the margarine then rub into the flour until it resembles breadcrumbs. Stir in the sugar then use a little water to bind it into pastry. Roll the pastry out on a floured surface. Turn the pie dish upside-down on top of the pastry and cut around it, leaving a ½ inch (1.5 cm) margin. Re-roll the pastry if necessary and cut around the upturned pie dish again (without leaving a margin) to make a lid for the pie. Carefully move the pastry base into the pie dish. Now add the cherry filling. Put the lid on the pie and crimp around the edge of the pie with finger and thumb to seal the lid onto the pie. If you have any remaining off-cuts of pastry then use these to make a cherry decoration for the lid of the pie and "glue" it on with a little egg or milk. Make a couple of air vents in the lid with a sharp knife. Glaze the whole lid with egg or milk then bake the pie in the oven at 180 °C, 350 °F, gas mark 3 for half an hour. Cool on a wire rack.

Storage
The pie filling can be preserved either by pouring it into a warmed jar whilst it is still hot and sealing the jar immediately, or by allowing it to cool and freezing it. Once the pie is made it will keep in an airtight container in a refrigerator for about 3 days. Alternatively, freeze the pie once it has cooled. Remove it from the freezer after about an hour or two and cut it into portions, bag them and freeze them separately.

Usage
Eat as a dessert either hot or cold with cream or custard.

Courgettes with Oregano

Ingredients (serves 1 or 2)
Oil (for frying)
1 medium onion
2 to 3 courgettes
1 garlic clove
3 tbsp stock
2 sprigs oregano
Salt and pepper

Equipment
Frying pan and spatula.

Method
Heal the oil in a frying pan. Chop the onions finely and fry until soft. Cut the courgettes into rounds and finely chop the garlic. Add the courgettes and garlic to the frying pan and fry until the courgettes are just turning brown on each side. Pour on the stock and the oregano and season. Simmer for 5 to 8 minutes until the liquid has almost gone. Serve immediately.

Usage
As a side dish for 2 or as the basis of a vegetarian meal for 1.

Broad Beans with Bacon

Ingredients (serves 1 or 2)
Oil (for frying)
1 medium onion
1 rasher of bacon
3 oz (85 g) broad beans
1 small little gem lettuce
5 tbsp stock
Freshly ground black pepper

Equipment
Saucepan and spatula.

Method
Heat the oil in a saucepan. Finely chop the onions and bacon and fry until just cooked. Add the broad beans and finely shredded lettuce, cover and cook for 4 to 5 minutes, stirring occasionally. Pour over the stock and season with pepper. Cook for 15 to 20 minutes over a low heat, stirring occasionally. Serve immediately.

Usage
As a side dish for 1 or 2 people.

Subsequent years

Things to do

Asparagus
The traditional day to stop cutting asparagus is mid-summer's day (21st June) but you should certainly stop cutting asparagus tips by the end of the month and allow ferns to develop. Over cutting now will result in a low yield of very spindly stems next year. Keep a check on asparagus beetle, as it will be in full swing by now. Asparagus beetle larvae, little black grubs, may also appear now and should be squashed.

Things to expect

Garlic
Over wintered garlic may well develop rust during June. Although it looks unpleasant, it does not affect the crop in anyway and can be ignored. Some garlic, particularly certain varieties, is prone to bolt at this time of year. Snap the flower stem off and use the garlic "in the green", as it won't store well.

Fruit
Don't be surprised if plum, apple and pear trees shed some small fruit in the next couple of months. This is perfectly normal and is the tree's way of lighting its load. In fact, if you have a very heavy crop it is worth while removing any damaged or distorted fruit yourself and discarding it. If a tree produces a very heavy crop one year, it will generally produce a lighter crop the following year to compensate and eventually your tree will become pretty much biennial.

Spring onions
Autumn sown spring onions may also bolt now but it is unlikely to affect all your plants. Snap off the flower stalks and use those bulbs next.

Herbs
Woody herbs such as sage, thyme and rosemary will flower in June. They all have beautiful flowers and although the foliage tends to become neglected by the plant whilst it flowers, it is well worth letting them do so as they look wonderful and the bees absolutely love them too.

Things to harvest
Garlic
Japanese onions
Spring onions
Autumn planted onions

In the Kitchen

Stir-fried Chicken with Mangetout and Spring Onions

Ingredients (serves 2)
For the stir fry:
2 chicken breasts

Mangetout (enough for two e.g. 5 to 8 oz, 140-225 g)
Oil for frying
1 garlic clove
1 inch (2.5 cm) piece of root ginger
3 to 4 spring onions

For the marinade:
1 tsp cornflour
1 tbsp soy sauce
1 tsp sherry
1 tsp olive oil

For the sauce:
1 tsp cornflour
4 fl oz (115 ml) chicken stock
2 tbsp oyster sauce

To serve:
6 oz (170 g) brown rice or 7 oz (200g) white rice

Equipment
Dish for marinating, bowl, grater, knife, 2 saucepans (for mangetout and rice), frying plan, slotted spoon, spatula, and sieve.

Method
Cut the chicken into strips and place in a dish. Add the marinade ingredients, combine and leave for about half an hour. In a bowl, combine the ingredients for the sauce. Finely chop the garlic, grate the ginger and cut the spring onions into long lengths. Put the rice on to boil. In the meantime, trim the mangetout and plunge into lightly salted, boiling water. Bring back to the boil, drain and refresh with cold water. Heat the oil in a frying plan and quickly fry the chicken pieces until browned all over. Remove the chicken and set aside. Add the mangetout, garlic and ginger to the frying pan and stir-fry for 1 to 2 minutes. Remove and set aside. Add the spring onions to the pan and stir-fry for 1 to 2 minutes. Return the chicken and stir-fry until cooked through. Pour in the sauce, reduce the heat and cook until the sauce thickens. Add the mangetout and heat through. Drain the rice and serve immediately.

Usage
As a meal for two.

July

By July things should be in full swing and you should be enjoying a variety of fruit and vegetables from your plot. In a way it is the best time of year because you are getting the most from your plot whilst having to do very little work on it. That is not to say that you can sit back and relax...

Every year

Things to do

Autumn/winter crops

Now is the time to start thinking about the crops you will want to sow at the end of the summer for use in the autumn, winter or spring. If you previously used seed catalogues to order from then these companies will probably automatically send you a copy of their autumn catalogue to look at. Some seeds, such as carrots, beetroot and winter salads will need to be sown at the end of July or during August. Others, such as garlic and onions will need to be planted out in October. As an easier (but more expensive) alternative to seeds, many crops can be bought as "starter" plants now. These are particularly useful if you were not organised enough earlier to sow the plants you needed or had some disaster that destroyed them. It is also a good time to think about and order any fruit trees or bushes if you didn't get round to it in the winter. These can be planted from November and information on varieties can be found in the November chapter. Everything you order should be delayed for dispatch until the correct time of year so don't worry about making a prompt order now. In fact, it is probably best to get your order in now so that you get your seeds in time for sowing and you can be sure that you will get your choice of fruit or whatever.

In a way, these are the most important crops of the year. It really is relatively easy to grow food for the summer and to have an abundance of it. It is slightly more of a challenge to grow things for winter or spring but very worthwhile as this is the leanest time of year and when things are at their most expensive in the shops. The other useful thing about growing more crops at this time of year is that the new crop will occupy empty space made vacant by earlier crops, making excellent use of your plot.

The crops you might like to consider are as follows:

Beetroot
Beetroot can be sown in July to provide a crop throughout the winter. They stand well in the ground all winter, although the foliage goes soggy when frosted. By removing the foliage after frost the roots will stand without damage and can be harvested fresh when required.

Broccoli and Kale
Broccoli and kale are particularly useful because they can be harvested, depending on variety, from December to March – just when you really need some fresh vegetables. They are also quite abundant and one of the few things you might have a glut of at that time of year. If you haven't sown seeds for these yet you might just be able to sow some at the beginning of this month or you can buy them as starter plants.

Broad beans
Some varieties of broad beans are very hardy and will survive the winter to give you an early crop of broad beans next year. It can be a matter of chance whether the plants survive the winter but in general they should do, even without cloche protection. The beans should then be ready approximately two weeks earlier than beans sown in the spring and tend to be less prone to blackfly damage because they crop before blackfly become a problem. I wouldn't consider autumn-sown broad beans as a replacement for spring ones but you may consider it worth the effort for that additional, earlier crop.

Carrots
Carrots sown in July will mature in time to give a reasonable root before they stop growing over winter. They stand in the ground well, although they are prone to damage from slugs etc. but it is nice to have a supply of fresh carrots all winter. They will bolt in the spring so should be used up before March. Carrots can also be sown under fleece in October to give an earlier than normal crop of carrots in the spring.

Garlic
Unless your soil becomes particularly boggy during the winter, I would recommend planting garlic cloves in the autumn. They seem to be much more successful if planted at this time of year rather than in the spring. In fact, spring sown garlic often develop one small bulb rather than splitting into cloves and it is said that garlic needs a period of cold to develop properly.

Japanese onions

I would recommend sowing some of these in August. They are ready even before autumn planted onion sets and seem to stand the winter better too. Because they are sown from seed they tend to give a much wider range of bulb size, from shallot to large onion size but this too is handy for different culinary uses.

Leeks

Leeks are a winter essential but are amazingly slow growing. Ideally they should be sown in February or March and will not be ready for harvesting until the winter. If you haven't already sown and planted your leeks then you can buy starter plants for them although they are generally expensive and you may not consider them economical. Seeds sown during July directly in the ground can go on to produce mini leeks before bolting in the spring. These can be very handy and are quite fashionable!

Onions

Autumn planted onion sets are something of a gamble. I have tried them several times, sometimes very successfully and sometimes to the point where I don't think I'll bother again. It seems to depend very much on the variety used and the winter weather conditions. It is certainly nicer to plant onion sets in the autumn, when it is not so cold, than in February and it does give a significantly earlier crop which can be very useful. However, the bulbs can easily rot in cold damp conditions and there can be many spaces come the spring.

Oriental leaves/winter salads

There is a whole selection of different and unusual salad leaves that stand remarkably well throughout the winter, most without cloche protection. They can be picked as and when you need them and provide salads throughout the hungry gap.

Spinach

This keeps going all winter and into early spring and leaves can be harvested as and when required without significantly damaging the plant.

Spring onions

These are definitely worth growing, providing small salad onions throughout the winter and larger ones in the spring.

Turnips
These are a good winter crop and even if you are not keen or sure about the taste, they are ideal in casseroles, curries and pies where they provide bulkiness without having an obvious flavour. Turnips can be sown in July.

Carrots and beetroot
Continue to thin these crops as the roots grow.

Cucumbers
These will grow best and take up less room if supported, so tie these to canes as they grow.

Garlic
Harvest all garlic by the end of July. The leaves should have died back by now. Harvest on a warm, sunny day and allow the bulbs to dry in the sun. They can then be stored in single layers in boxes or can be tied into strings or plaited.

Peppers, aubergines and melons
Remove fleece covering from these to allow more water in, to allow insects to pollinate the flowers and to let the sun ripen any fruit that is produced.

Tomatoes
Continue to remove side-shoots on cordon tomatoes and tie the central stem to its support as necessary. This job needs to be done at least once a week otherwise the side shoots will become large stems before you know what has happened. It is important to prevent cordons from becoming bushy because this reduces ventilation to the plant and leaves it open to blight.

Water
Continue to check plants for water stress and water as necessary.

Watercress
It is worth sowing another batch of watercress during July. If you sowed some earlier it will probably have bolted and gone over by now. Even if it hasn't, it is still best to discard the plant, clean out the container and replace it frequently because standing water can become a breeding ground for unpleasant bugs. Because of the warm conditions in July, the freshly sown seeds should germinate quickly and grow rapidly so you should have another just about edible crop within a fortnight.

Weeds

With the warm weather the weeds will grow rapidly. Try to keep on top of the weeds. If you have any areas of bare soil then cover them up with black/opaque plastic, cardboard or carpet to keep the weeds suppressed.

Things to expect

Asparagus

Continue to look out for asparagus beetle during July and expect to see more grub-like black larvae.

Broad beans

Your broad bean harvest will probably come to an end by the end of the month. Even if beans remain on the plant into August, they will be tough and not very pleasant to eat. If you didn't spray your broad beans earlier then you should see quite a few ladybirds and their larvae on the plants during August. The plants might develop chocolate spot on their leaves now but, although unsightly, it does not seem to significantly harm the plants and no action is necessary.

Calabrese

Depending on the variety and when you planted them, you may begin to see flower heads beginning to form during July, although they will probably not be big enough to harvest until next month. Watch out for butterfly eggs on the underside of the leaves – these will develop into caterpillars next month if not dispatched now.

Cucumbers

Cucumbers should start to form fruit and will be ready for harvesting by the end of the month.

Fruit

Summer strawberries will finish cropping by the end of the month.

Onions and shallots

The foliage will still be green during July but the bulbs will be pretty much full size by now. They can be harvested now as and when you wish to eat them but don't harvest them for storage until the foliage has died back; this won't be until the end of August or the beginning of September.

Peas and mangetout
Expect to find more maggots inside pea pods when you shell them now. The peas and mangetout will be becoming old and less pleasant to eat and the plants will start to die back. The whole crop will be finished by the end of the month.

Potatoes
Depending on your soil conditions and the variety of potato, you may have damage on potatoes that you lift during July.

Pumpkins
This is when you discover whether you gave your pumpkins enough space when you planted them. The foliage really takes off during July and will swamp anything that is planted too close to it. It is possible to attempt some sort of training of pumpkins, although they are not particularly co-operative and are best when they have plenty of space. If they are too close this year then make a mental note and give them more space next year. You will probably find that the plants nearby suffer rather than the pumpkin.

Tomatoes
Tomatoes should be well in flower and fruit should continue to develop during July.

Things to harvest
Beetroot
Broad beans
Calabrese (possibly)
Carrots
Cherries
Courgettes
Cucumber
Currants
Florence fennel
Garlic (all)
Gherkins
Gooseberries (green and red)
Mangetout
Onions
Peas
Potatoes
Raspberries
Shallots
Spring onions

Strawberries

Harvesting Techniques

Calabrese
Wait until the central flower head is a good size before harvesting it but remove it before the buds begin to swell and loosen. Using a sharp knife, cut the head off with an inch or so of stem. Once this is removed, smaller side shoots will begin to form that can be harvested later.

Florence fennel
If the ground is soft and damp enough it should be possible to pull a fennel bulb directly out of the ground with a little bit of rocking and twisting. It does have quite a large taproot on it so if it is particularly reluctant to give, use a small fork or try cutting it off at ground level. Once out of the ground the taproot and the ferns can be cut off and composted. If your germination rate was good then the first bulbs you harvest should be those growing close to others so that you thin the row out and allow the remaining bulbs to expand.

Gherkins and Cucumber
As with all cucurbits, gherkins and cucumbers can be harvested by simply twisting the fruit at its stem or by cutting the stem. These plants are less spiky than courgette plants so are easier to tackle, although the gherkin fruit itself is surprisingly spiky. Any spines on the fruit will be removed when the fruit is washed.

Cooking tips

Calabrese
Ideally calabrese should be steamed (see Equipment and Techniques chapter). Whether boiling or steaming, large heads should be cut into smaller florets for faster and more convenient cooking.

Florence fennel
For the strongest aniseed flavour, fennel can be eaten raw, for example, in a salad. Fennel can also be boiled fairly easily by cutting into pieces and boiling in lightly salted water for 5 to 10 minutes, depending on how crisp you like it. To roast fennel wrap it up in some foil with a small amount of oil with some seasoning and cook it at the same time as your Sunday roast.

Freezing

Calabrese and **fennel** can be frozen relatively successfully if cut into pieces and blanched first (see Equipment and Techniques chapter). **Cucumber** absolutely cannot stand freezing. See June for freezing tips on strawberries, peas, mangetout and broad beans.

Pickling

Gherkins can be pickled and the recipe is given below.

Drying
Garlic will store well into next year if the foliage has completely died back before lifting and if it is allowed to dry in the sun before being moved to a cool, dry place. If any of the bulbs bolted, don't attempt to store these but use them up first instead.

In Storage

In the freezer
Broad beans
Peas
Ice cream

In the store cupboard
Pickled beetroot
Chutney
Jam

In the kitchen

Pickled Gherkins

Gherkins can be pickled in malt or pickling vinegar. The only difference between the two vinegars is the addition of spices to the pickling vinegar, which I believe makes the gherkins too tangy to be pleasant but which others might like.

Ingredients
Gherkins
Salt

Water
Malt vinegar

Equipment
Kitchen paper, greaseproof paper, jars.

Method
Wash the gherkins to remove any residual soil and the spines. If small enough, keep the gherkins whole; if larger then slice into discs. Pack into a suitable sized jar, sprinkling on salt as you go. Be generous with the salt and don't worry about the taste, as it will be washed off. Pour in the water and seal the jar overnight. Drain the gherkins, rinse well under running water and dry on kitchen paper. Also rinse and dry the lid and jar. Pack the gherkins back into the jar and fill to the top with vinegar. Place a ball of greaseproof paper in the neck of the jar to keep the gherkins submerged then seal and label the jar.

Storage
Store for 2 to 3 months to allow the flavours to develop and use within a year.

Usage
Can be used as an accompaniment to cold meats. Can be used on burgers, in sandwiches or as a dip (see recipes below).

Dill Pickle

Ingredients (makes 4 to 6 jars)
6 small cucumbers or large gherkins or 12 small gherkins
16 fl oz (475 ml) water
1¾ pints (1 litre) white wine vinegar
4 oz (115 g) salt
3 bay leaves
3 tbsp dill seed
2 garlic cloves, sliced

Equipment
Saucepan, jars.

Method
Wash the cucumbers to remove soil and spines. Cut the cucumbers into slices or leave small gherkins whole. In a saucepan, heat the water, vinegar and salt to boiling then immediately remove from the

heat. In suitable jars, layer the sliced cucumbers with the garlic, dill and bay until the jar is well packed. Pour the warm liquid into the jars and seal immediately.

Storage
Leave it to mature for at least a week before using but is best left for a month for the flavours to develop. Use within a year.

Uses
Excellent served with hamburgers, cold meat or in canapés and snacks.

Gherkin and Mayonnaise Dip

Ingredients
2 tbsp mayonnaise
1 whole pickled (or fresh) gherkin or 4 to 5 slices
3 chives
Freshly ground black pepper

Equipment
Small dip bowl.

Method
Place the mayonnaise in a suitable dish. Rinse any excess vinegar from the pickled gherkin and dry then chop into very small pieces. Snip the chives into small pieces with scissors. Add all the ingredients to the mayonnaise and stir until well combined.

Storage
Store in a covered container in a refrigerator for 1 to 2 days.

Usage
As a dip or as a sandwich spread.

Gherkin Tzatziki

Ingredients
2 tbsp natural yoghurt
1 whole pickled (or fresh) gherkin or 4 to 5 slices
¼ garlic clove
2 mint leaves

Equipment
Small dip bowl.

Method
Place the yoghurt in a suitable dish. Rinse any excess vinegar from the pickled gherkin and chop it into very small pieces. Finely chop the garlic and mint leaves. Add all ingredients to the yoghurt and stir until well combined.

Storage
Store in a covered container in a refrigerator for 1 to 2 days.

Usage
As a dip or accompaniment.

Pea and Bacon Soup

By the end of July any peas left on your plants will be getting old and starchy and will not be particularly pleasant to eat. This recipe makes use of those peas. By the end of July your celery plants might not be big enough to harvest the stems but it should be possible to harvest either leaf celery or a few leaves from conventional celery to give the required flavour. If that is not the case then use a teaspoon of celery salt instead. When choosing jars for storing the soup, try to find suitable jars that are approximately equivalent to one or two servings for convenience.

Ingredients (makes 4 to 5 jars)
For stock (making 1 pint (500 ml)):
1 onion
2 pieces of celery
1 carrot
Thyme, bay and rosemary
Water

For soup:
Oil (for frying)
1 onion (small to medium)
1 large garlic clove
13 oz (370 g) potatoes
2 handfuls of celery leaves
1 lb (450 g) peas
4 rashers of smoked bacon back

Water
Salt and pepper

Equipment
Large saucepan, spatula, blender/food processor, ladle, jam funnel, 4 to 5 jars.

Method
If necessary prepare the stock (see Equipment and Techniques chapter), or use 2 prepared jars. Heat some oil in the bottom of a large saucepan or preserving pan. Chop the onions and fry until soft. Add coarsely chopped garlic and fry for a further 1 to 2 minutes. Peel and dice the potatoes and add them to the pan with the celery leaves and stock. Simmer for 20 minutes. In the meantime grill the bacon until cooked. Remove 3 rashers from the grill and set aside. Return the other rasher to the grill and cook until crispy. Cut the bacon into small pieces and snip the crispy rasher into tiny pieces using scissors. Add the peas and the 3 rashers of bacon strips to the stock and bring back to the boil. Simmer for 5 minutes. Remove the soup from the heat then puree it in a blender in batches until smooth. Pour into a clean saucepan and add water as necessary to thin. Add the crispy bacon pieces and season to taste. Bring back to the boil then ladle into serving bowls or hot jars and seal immediately.

Storage
Once the soup has cooled the safety button should have become depressed again. If it has, then the soup can be stored for several months, if not then use within 3 days.

Usage
As a filling small meal such as lunch or a light dinner, served with bread. If correctly bottled it can be stored until winter when it is a very welcome winter filler.

Chicken and Potato Bake

Ingredients (serves 2)
Oil (for frying)
2 skinless chicken breasts
4 to 5 spring onions
2 to 3 carrots
1 pint (600 ml) stock
8 oz (225 g) small, waxy potatoes

1 to 2 garlic cloves
Salt and pepper
Fresh herbs (such as rosemary, thyme, sage and bay)

Equipment
Large deep frying pan, potato peeler, tongs, spatula, knife, large spoon and casserole dish with lid.

Method
To prepare vegetables:
Top and tail the spring onions and cut into rounds. Wash and peel the carrots and cut into rounds. Wash the potatoes but leave unpeeled and whole. Remove herb leaves from the stalks and discard any tough stems then tear the leaves into pieces. Peel and finely chop the garlic.

To prepare the bake:
Preheat oven to 190 °C, 375 °F, gas mark 5. Heat some oil in a frying plan then add the chicken breasts. Fry for 5 to 8 minutes until brown all over. Lift the chicken from the pan and set aside. Add the spring onions and carrots and fry for 3 to 4 minutes. Return the chicken to the pan, and add the stock, potatoes, herbs and garlic. Season and bring to the boil. Transfer all the ingredients to the casserole dish and cover. Place in an oven and cook for 40 to 50 minutes until the potatoes are tender.

Usage
Serves 2 as a complete meal.

Subsequent years

Things to do

Herbs
Biennial herbs such as parsley will bolt now if 2 years old. Now is the time to replace these herbs with new ones.

Garlic
Harvest all garlic (see above).

Spring onions
Autumn sown spring onions will be coming to the end of their usefulness and will be developing large bulbs. Try to use them up this month.

Japanese onions
The foliage on these will start to die back now. As soon as the foliage is dry, the bulbs can be lifted and stored.

Things to harvest
Autumn planted onions
Cherries
Currants
Garlic
Gooseberries
Japanese onions
Raspberries
Spring onions
Tayberries

Harvesting techniques

Cherries
Some people net their cherry trees to stop birds from pinching the ripe fruit. However, sometimes birds get themselves caught up in the netting and have to be rescued, which is distressing all round. It is perhaps easier to pick the fruit when it is still slightly under ripe and allow it to ripen fully on a sunny windowsill. You may lose the odd cherry here and there with this method but not enough to worry about.

Currants
If possible this is best done sat down. Wait until all or most of the currants are ripe, wedge a container between your knees and strip the berries into it. Watch out for ants, as these will be crawling over the fruit – particularly on blackcurrants.

Gooseberries
These are the most problematic of the soft fruit. Firstly, unless you have red gooseberries, it is difficult to tell when the fruit is ripe. You may find that the birds will tell you by starting to eat them or the occasional fruit might split or be damaged on a thorn when ripe. They should be slightly springy between your fingers with prominent veining. Don't worry too much about picking under ripe berries for jelly and jam making as this helps it to set. The next problem with most gooseberry varieties is the abundance of long, sharp thorns that can make picking the fruit a painful affair. There is no easy way round this and you just have to be careful or wear thick gloves.

Raspberries and Tayberries

These are very easy to harvest and quite a nice height to pick as they don't require much bending. If the berries are ripe they can easily be pulled off the plant between finger and thumb, leaving the hull behind on the bush.

Preserving Tips

Freezing

All soft fruit can be frozen successfully without blanching for use later in jams etc. It can be useful to freeze fruit as it ripens and accumulate it in the freezer until you have a large enough batch for jam making. Do not freeze fruit if you are intending to use it in ice cream because it would have to be refrozen (without cooking) once in the ice cream. The fruit is mushy once thawed so is not suited for eating in the same way as fresh fruit.

In the kitchen

As with strawberries (see June), I have tried to provide a variety of different ideas for using July's soft fruit to create interest and to cater for all tastes.

Raspberry Ice cream

As for strawberry ice cream (see June) but with 12 oz (340 g) of raspberries instead of strawberries.

Raspberry Jam

Below is a recipe for raspberry jam. Please read the section of jam making in the Equipment and Techniques chapter if you haven't already done so. Some people find the large pips in raspberries a little unpleasant in jam. If this is the case then I suggest you make raspberry jelly instead, which is seedless (see recipe below), with or without the port.

Ingredients (makes 5 to 6 jars)
3 lb (1400 g) raspberries (not too ripe!)
3 lb (1400 g) sugar

NB: Every pound of raspberries requires 1 lb sugar.

Equipment
Preserving pan, ovenproof dish, wooden spoon, ladle, jam funnel, 5 to 6 jars.

Method
Place raspberries in the preserving pan and heat very gently until the juices start to run. Leave to simmer for 20 minutes until the fruit is cooked, shaking the pan or gently stirring occasionally. Meanwhile warm the sugar. Once the fruit is cooked, add the sugar and stir over a low heat until the sugar is completely dissolved. Bring to the boil and boil rapidly until the setting point is reached. Transfer into warmed jars and seal immediately.

Storage
In a cool, dry place for up to 2 years.

Usage
On toast, in cakes and other desserts (see recipe below).

Raspberry Chewies

Ingredients (makes 12)
2 oz (55 g) butter
3 tbsp raspberry jam
2 oz (55 g) marshmallows
4 oz (110 g) cornflakes

Equipment
Saucepan, spoon, paper cases.

Method
In a saucepan melt together the butter, jam and marshmallows. Stir in the cornflakes until well combined. Spoon into paper cases and chill.

Storage
Store in a cool place in an airtight container for 1 to 3 days. By the 3rd day the cornflakes become very soft.

Usage
This is a very sweet dessert so is more popular with children than adults. Makes good party food.

Raspberry and Port Jelly

Before making this recipe, please read the section on jelly making in the Equipment and Techniques chapter. The alcohol in the port evaporates off when added to the hot jelly so the resulting jelly has the taste of port but is non-alcoholic.

Ingredients (makes 2 to 3 jars)
2½ lb (1100 kg) raspberries
About 14 oz (400 g) sugar
1½ tbsp port

NB: Every pound of raspberries requires 5½ oz sugar and two thirds of tbsp port.

Equipment
Jelly sieve or alternative (see Equipment and Techniques chapter), bowl, ovenproof dish, preserving pan, ladle, jam funnel, 2 to 3 jars.

Method
Squash or pulp the raspberries then pour into a jelly bag over a bowl and leave to drip overnight (do not squeeze otherwise jelly will be cloudy). Measure the liquid and for each pint (660 ml) weigh 1 lb (450 g) sugar. Warm the sugar in the oven. Pour the liquid into a preserving pan and add the warmed sugar. Heat gently until all the sugar is dissolved. Bring to the boil and boil rapidly for 5 to 9 minutes until the setting point is reached. Remove from the heat and stir in the port. Transfer into warmed jars and seal immediately.

Storage
For up to 2 years in a cool, dark place.

Usage
As you would normally use raspberry jam.

Redcurrant, Raspberry and Sherry Jelly

This is a good recipe if you have an abundance of redcurrants but only a few raspberries. Please read the Equipment and Techniques chapter on jelly making if you haven't already done so. Redcurrants are high pectin fruit so it is easy to get this to set and in fact, it can turn out a bit rubbery if boiled for too long!

Ingredients (makes 1 to 2 jars)
2¼ lb (1000g) redcurrants
10½ oz (300 g) raspberries
11 fl oz (300 ml) water
About 1 lb (450 g) sugar
2 tbsp sherry

Equipment
Preserving pan, jelly bag, bowl, ovenproof dish, ladle, jam funnel, 1 to 2 jars.

Method
Pick over the redcurrants and raspberries and wash. Place the fruit in a preserving pan with the water and bring to the boil. Simmer for 10 to 15 minutes until the fruit is soft and pulpy. Pour into a jelly bag over a bowl and leave to drip overnight. Measure the juice and for each pint (600 ml) weigh 1 lb (450 g) sugar. Warm the sugar in a cool oven. Pour the liquid into the preserving pan and add the sugar, stirring constantly until it has completely dissolved. Bring it to the boil and boil rapidly for 7 to 10 minutes until it reaches its setting point. Remove from the heat, stir in the sherry then pour into warmed jars and seal immediately.

Storage
Store in a cool dark place for up to 2 years.

Usage
Although this jelly can be used in the same way as any conventional jam, it is best used as an accompaniment to meat such as duck or lamb (see recipe below).

Duck with Herbs and Red Fruit Jelly

Ingredients (serves 2)
2 duck breasts
Salt and pepper
1 tbsp hoi sin sauce
2 sprigs each rosemary, sage, thyme and chives
1 tbsp redcurrant, raspberry and sherry jelly

Equipment
Fork, kitchen towel, roasting tin with rack

Method
Preheat oven to 190 ºC, 375 ºF, gas mark 6. Prick the skin of the duck breasts with a fork and rub in salt. Turn the breasts skin side down onto a piece of kitchen towel. Season the underside of the breast with salt and pepper and smear with hoi sin sauce. Tear the sage, rosemary, thyme and chives and press onto the sauce. Place the breasts skin side up on a rack over a roasting tin and remove the kitchen towel. Cook in the centre of the oven for 30 minutes. Take out and rest for 5 minutes before serving with the red jelly.

Usage
Serves 2 as an evening meal with suitable accompaniment such as new potatoes or rice, peas or mangetout.

Blackcurrant Muffins

Ingredients
8 oz (225 g) plain flour
1 tsp baking powder
Pinch of salt
2 tbsp wheatgerm
3 oz (85 g) soft dark brown sugar
6 fl oz (170 ml) milk
2½ fl oz (70 ml) sunflower oil
1 egg
6 oz (170 g) blackcurrants
2 oz (55 g) caster sugar
1 tbsp water

Equipment
Muffin tin and paper muffin cases, large bowl, sieve, wooden spoon, small bowl, fork, small saucepan and wire rack.

Method
Preheat an oven to 220 ºC, 425 ºF, gas mark 7 and put 9 muffin cases into the muffin tin. Sift the flour, baking powder and salt into a bowl. Stir in the wheatgerm and sugar. Add the milk and mix until it becomes a thick batter. In another bowl, beat the egg into the oil then add it to the batter and mix until smooth. Pick over the blackcurrants and place them in a saucepan. Add the sugar and water and very slowly bring it to the boil then remove it from the heat. Spoon the blackcurrant mix into the batter, leaving behind any excess liquid. Stir the batter until it is evenly pink. Spoon the mixture into the muffin

cases until each is about three-quarters full. If your muffin tin has more than 9 holes, pour a small amount of water into each remaining hole to allow for more even cooking. Bake in the oven for 20 minutes until well risen, golden brown and springy. Leave to cool in the tin for 5 minutes then cool completely on a wire rack.

Storage
Store in an airtight container for up to 5 days.

Usage
As a snack or dessert. If it is not sweet enough for your taste, open up the muffin and smear with jam.

Blackcurrant Crumble

Ingredients (serves 4 to 6)
For the filling:
1 lb (450 g) blackcurrants
2 tbsp caster sugar

For the crumble:
4 oz (110 g) wholemeal flour
4 oz (110 g) oats
1 tsp baking powder
3 oz (85 g) butter
5 oz (140g) soft dark brown sugar

Equipment
Bowl and ovenproof dish.

Method
Preheat oven to 180 °C, 350 °F, gas mark 4. Place the flour, oats and baking powder in a bowl. Chop up the butter and add it to the dry ingredients. Rub the butter in with your fingertips until the mixture is crumbly and resembles breadcrumbs. Add the sugar and combine. Pick over and wash the blackcurrants. Place the fruit in a suitable dish and sprinkle over the caster sugar. Sprinkle the crumble mix over the fruit and spread out evenly. Bake on a high shelf in the oven for 30 to 40 minutes until the topping is slightly brown. Serve immediately.

Storage
This dish is best served immediately although it can be stored overnight in the refrigerator then reheated the next day. It can be

made in advance and frozen. However, it is more economical on freezer space to freeze the fruit separately, defrost it and use it in this recipe.

Usage
Serve hot with cream or custard as a filling dessert.

Blackcurrant Cheesecake

Ingredients
For base:
5¾ oz (165 g) whole hazelnuts
3 oz (85g) plain flour
Pinch of salt
2 oz (55 g) butter
5½ oz (155 g) soft light brown sugar

For Filling:
2 oz (55 g) caster sugar
6 oz (170 g) soft cheese (cream cheese)
1 egg
4 fl oz (115 ml) whipping cream

For topping:
12 oz (340 g) blackcurrants
1 tbsp honey
8 oz (225 g) granulated sugar

Equipment
Blender, 2 bowls, sieve, wooden spoon, 9 inch (23 cm) pie dish (at least 1½ in, 4 cm deep), small saucepan, whisk and wire rack.

Method
To make the base, place the hazelnuts in the blender and process until finely ground. Put the ground hazelnuts in a bowl, sift in the flour and salt and stir. In another bowl, cream together the butter and brown sugar until smooth. Add the butter mix to the nut mix until well combined. Grease the pie dish and spoon the mixture into it. Press it evenly against the bottom and sides to form a case. Cover and refrigerate for 30 minutes. Preheat an oven to 180 °C, 350 °F, gas mark 3. In the meantime prepare the topping by placing the blackcurrants, honey and sugar in a saucepan. Cook on a low heat, stirring occasionally for 5 to 7 minutes. Remove from the heat and set

aside. Next bake the base for 15 minutes and leave it to cool on a rack. To make the filling, beat together the cream cheese and sugar until light and fluffy. Add the egg and whipping cream and beat until smooth. Pour the filling into the cool base and spread evenly. Bake for 20 to 25 minutes until just set. Cool the cheesecake completely on a rack then cover it and refrigerate for at least an hour. To finish, pour the blackcurrant mix over the top.

Storage
If using fresh, eat within 1 to 2 days. To freeze, place in a freezer (uncovered) for 3 hours until partially frozen. Remove from the freezer and cut into portions, ensuring each piece can be removed from the dish individually. Cover and return to the freezer until completely frozen. To defrost, remove individual portions as required and thaw for 1 to 2 hours at room temperature before serving.

Usage
Serve at room temperature as a dessert.

Blackcurrant Jam

This is a very easy jam to make because blackcurrants are high in pectin and the jam sets well. Please read the jam making section of the Equipment and Techniques chapter before making this recipe if you haven't already done so.

Ingredients (makes 6 to 8 jars)
4 lb (1800 g) blackcurrants
2½ pints (1400 ml) water
4 lb (1800 g) sugar

NB: Every pound of blackcurrants requires 12½ fl oz water and 1 lb sugar

Equipment
Preserving pan, wooden spoon, ovenproof dish, ladle, jam funnel and 6 to 8 jars.

Method
Pick over the blackcurrants but there is no need to wash the fruit. Put them into a preserving pan with the water and bring it to the boil. Simmer for 40 to 50 minutes, stirring occasionally, until the skins are tender. In the meantime, warm the sugar. When the fruit is cooked,

add the sugar to the blackcurrants and stir over a low heat until the sugar is completely dissolved. Boil rapidly for 6 to 8 minutes until the setting point is reached. Skim off any scum, then ladle into jars and seal immediately.

Storage
For up to 2 years in a cool, dry place.

Usage
On toast, in cakes and tarts and for flapjacks (see below).

Blackcurrant and Raisin Flapjacks

Ingredients (makes 12)
4¾ oz (135 g) margarine
5¼ oz (150 g) blackcurrant jam
8 oz (225 g) oats
Pinch of salt
¾ oz (20 g) sunflower seeds
1¾ oz (50 g) raisins

Equipment
9-inch (23-cm) square cake tin, large saucepan, wooden spoon.

Method
Preheat oven to 190 °C, 375 °F, gas mark 5. Line and grease the cake tin. In a large saucepan, gently melt together the margarine and the jam. Remove from the heat and add the oats, salt, seeds and raisins. Stir well until fully combined. Spoon into the cake tin and press down well with wetted fingers. Bake for 15 to 20 minutes until golden brown. Mark out to 12 pieces then allow it to cool completely in the tin.

Storage
Store in an airtight container for up to a week.

Usage
As a filling, nutritious snack.

Blackcurrant Jelly

If you hate seeds in your jam then try this jelly instead but bear in mind that it does not make as many jars for the same quantity of fruit. Please read the jelly making section of the Equipment and Techniques chapter before making this recipe if you haven't already done so.

Ingredients (makes 3 to 4 jars)
4 lb (1800 g) blackcurrants
2 pints (1100 ml) water
About 2 lb sugar

NB: Every pound of blackcurrants requires ½ pint of water and approximately ½ pound sugar.

Equipment
Preserving pan, wooden spoon, jelly bag (or alternative), bowl, ovenproof dish, ladle, jam funnel, 3 to 4 jars.

Method
Pick over the blackcurrants. Put them into a preserving pan with the water and cook for 30 to 40 minutes until soft. Pour the fruit into a jelly bag and strain overnight without squeezing the bag. Measure the strained liquid and weigh 1 lb of sugar for every pint of liquid collected. (NB: retain the bag of fruit to use for making ice cream, see below.) Pour the liquid into a clean preserving pan and stir in the warmed sugar. Stir over a low heat until the sugar has completely dissolved then bring it to the boil and heat rapidly for 3 to 5 minutes until the setting point is reached. Skim off any scum, then ladle into jars and seal immediately.

Storage
Store in a cool, dry place for up to 2 years.

Usage
This jelly can be used as an alternative to blackcurrant jam as well as being used as an accompaniment to meat such as duck and lamb. It is also tasty mixed with natural yoghurt as a light dessert.

Blackcurrant Ice Cream

Rather than specially pureeing blackcurrants for this recipe, it can be useful to make this ice cream after making the blackcurrant jelly. In this case, instead of throwing away the fruit in the jelly bag, squeeze it over a bowl and use that as the puree in this recipe.

Ingredients
1 lb (450 g) blackcurrants
6 oz (170 g) sugar
5 fl oz (140 ml) water
½ pint (300 ml) double cream

Equipment
Pureeing equipment (see Equipment and Techniques chapter), 2 bowls, small saucepan, whisk, wooden spoon and plastic container.

Method
Puree the blackcurrants (see Equipment and Techniques chapter). Place the sugar and the water in a saucepan over a medium heat and stir until the sugar has dissolved. Bring to the boil and boil for 3 minutes. Remove from the heat and pour it into the pureed fruit and allow to cool slightly. In a separate bowl, whisk the cream until it starts to thicken. Fold the cream into the fruit mixture until evenly pink throughout. Pour the mixture into a suitable plastic container and place in the freezer for 3 hours; then remove the ice cream from the freezer, whisk again and return.

Storage
Store in the freezer for up to 3 months.

Usage
This is a very fruity but quite tart tasting ice cream. Some people would find it too sharp to eat by itself whilst others would enjoy its bite. It is probably best served as an accompaniment to a very sweet dessert such as a Pavlova where it contrasts well with the sweetness.

Gooseberry Jelly

This recipe is best made with red dessert gooseberries because it gives the jelly a very attractive colour. However, it can be made with green gooseberries, giving a slightly less attractive result. Please read the jelly making section of the Equipment and Techniques chapter before making this recipe if you haven't already done so.

Ingredients (makes about 1 jar)
2¼ lb (1000 g) red dessert gooseberries

16 fl oz (450 ml) water
About 8 oz sugar

Equipment
Preserving pan, wooden spoon, jelly bag, ovenproof dish, ladle, jam funnel and 1 jar.

Method
Place the gooseberries in a preserving pan with the water and cook for 30 to 40 minutes until soft and pulpy. Pour the fruit pulp into a jelly bag over a bowl and strain overnight. Measure the strained liquid and for every ½ pint (300 ml) weight out 8 oz (225 g) sugar. Warm the sugar then add it to the liquid and gently heat until all the sugar has dissolved. Boil rapidly for 3 to 4 minutes until the setting point is reached. Ladle into a warmed jar and seal immediately.

Storage
Store in a cool, dry place for up to 2 years.

Usage
This can be used as you would use any jam or jelly but is also an excellent accompaniment to smoked fish.

Summer Fruits in Cassis

Ingredients (2 to 3 jars)
1½ lb (700 g) soft summer fruit (e.g. blackcurrants, redcurrants, raspberries, small strawberries, or alpine strawberries)
9 oz (255 g) sugar
½ pint (250 ml) gin
2¼ fl oz (60 ml) cassis

Equipment
Bowl, wooden spoon, 2 to 3 jars.

Method
Pick over the fruit and carefully mix it together in a bowl with the sugar, trying not to squash any of it. Spoon the fruit into jars, packing it in well but without squashing it. Mix together the gin and cassis and pour it over the fruit. Seal and tilt the jars to remove any air bubbles.

Storage
Store for 2 to 3 months for flavours to develop, tilting occasionally to dissolve the sugar.

Usage
The alcoholic fruit can be used with or in desserts such as with ice cream, in pancakes or as a topping for meringue nests. In addition, the alcoholic liquid is a pleasant fruity drink. The fruit is especially good to use around Christmas for a festive taste of summer, although it needs to be served with something sweet or creamy to take away some of the sharpness.

August

If June is the strawberry and mangetout month then August is the apple and tomato month. This is the month when the savoury fruits (tomato, cucumber, aubergine, peppers) ripen. Where last month you might have spent a good deal of time making jams and desserts, this month you could spend a lot of your time making chutney, pickle, sauces and ketchup. It is also the point when your plot starts to go past its peak, soil becomes available and new crops need to be sown.

Every year

Things to do

Autumn crops

Sow autumn crops such as **carrots, beetroot, turnips, fennel, oriental leaves, spinach, winter salads, Japanese onions, and winter spring onions** into any free soil. Make sure the soil is broken into a fine tilth first, draw out a drill with a hoe, water, sow and cover over. Install slug protection measures. Carrots, beetroot, turnips and fennel should be sown at the beginning of August if you didn't manage to get it done at the end of July. The others can be sown towards the middle or end of the month.

Broccoli and Kale

Now is the time to plant out your winter brassicas such as sprouting broccoli and kale. This can be done on land previously occupied by potatoes, onions, shallots, garlic, broad beans, peas or mangetout. Adding lime and fertiliser will improve the soil. The soil should be firm to give the plants well anchored roots, so freshly dug ground needs to be compressed under foot. The new seedlings will need protection from pigeons and slugs, and will need to be watered well.

Potatoes

Finish harvesting first early potatoes, clear the plot, add fertiliser and rake over. This ground can now be used for new crops. If it is presently surplus to requirements, cover over with plastic, cardboard or carpet to stop weeds from growing. Watch for blight on main crop potatoes; it can be recognised by brown and black patches on the foliage. Remove the diseased foliage and discard by burning or throwing in the rubbish bin. Lift any tubers now and use as soon as possible.

Pumpkins

Your pumpkin plants will start to form fruit during August. Some may turn yellow and fall off when still very small because the flower wasn't fertilised. However, others will remain green and start to swell. You will need to decide how many pumpkins you want from each plant. Generally, the fewer fruit it has, the larger they grow. Each plant should be able to successfully grow 1 to 4 fruit. A nice idea to try with children is to gently score the surface of the fruit with their name or a design. As the fruit grows, the name heals over with a bubbly texture and expands with the fruit and each child has their own personalised fruit at the end. Bear in mind, however, that if something goes wrong with that fruit they will be hugely disappointed!

Shallots

Once the foliage has died back and dried, shallots can be lifted. Do this on a sunny, dry day and allow them to dry in the sun for a while before putting them into storage. They can be stored in open, shallow boxes or tied into strings. As you go, sort out any very small bulbs to use as pickling onions.

Soil

Now that the peas and mangetout are over and the last of the late broad beans are going that way too, the old plants need removing. Peas and beans are known as legumes and are unusual in that they have nodules on their roots full of nitrogen fixing bacteria. These bacteria are one of the few things that can extract nitrogen from the atmosphere and convert it to useful nitrates in the soil. This is a symbiotic relationship and the plants benefit from the extra nutrition they receive. Growing these crops is also, therefore, beneficial to the soil because it aids fertility. In order to preserve this useful asset, care should be taken when removing pea and bean crops to leave the roots behind in the soil.

Tomatoes

Continue to remove side shoots and tie the plants to canes as necessary. Once the second truss has formed fruit, water with a tomato feed. Watch for signs of blight, particularly if the weather has been warm and wet, not unusual in a British August. Blight can occur if the conditions are above 10 °C, with more than 75 % humidity and if the plants are wet for several hours, quite possible at this time of year. This is why it is better to apply water and liquid fertiliser to the roots rather than spray over the plant. Blight can be recognised by blackening of the leaves, stem or fruit. At the first sign of blight, remove any affected plants and spray the reminder with a copper-based fungicide and re-spray once a fortnight. If you object to using sprays then the plants will quickly succumb to blight. It is possible to pick the fruit whilst still green and make a green tomato chutney or similar. You could also try just removing affected parts of plants but this does not delay the problem for long. Any blighted plants should be thrown in the rubbish bin or burnt but not added to your compost bin because it will contaminate your compost. Tomatoes grown undercover don't tend to get blight as long as they aren't kept wet for long periods of time. Some outdoor tomatoes ripen earlier and can give you one truss of fruit before blight strikes.

Water
Check crops for water stress and wilting; water as necessary. Be aware that some fruit, such as tomatoes, will split if they get dry and then have a sudden drenching.

Weeds
Continue to weed as necessary to keep on top of the problem.

Things to expect

Asparagus
Asparagus beetle will still be present and may be causing some visible damage, leaving stripped stems.

Aubergines
Aubergines should continue to flower and form fruit throughout August. Mini aubergine varieties should form fruit big enough to harvest during this month but larger fruiting varieties may not be ready until next month.

Autumn crops
Autumn seeds should germinate within a week or two of being sown. Turnips will germinate very quickly, followed by beetroot, carrots then fennel.

Beans
Dwarf French beans will flower and form fruit towards the beginning of the month, slightly ahead of the climbing beans. Climbing beans should reach the top of their supports soon. They should be flowering by the beginning of the month and the formation of the first beans will quickly follow. This applies to lablab beans too.

Broccoli
Check the underside of broccoli leaves for caterpillars and remove them. You may find caterpillars in amongst your calabrese heads. Don't be surprised to find the odd boiled caterpillar in with your cooked vegetables!

Melons
Fruit should develop on melons this month but probably won't be ready to harvest yet.

Onions
Watch out for mildew on the foliage of onions. It will appear as a white powder and will quickly spread through your whole crop. It can be controlled in the same way as blight by using a copper-based fungicide. This once allowed me to rescue a crop of onions suffering from what an editor of Kitchen Garden Magazine described as one of the worst cases of mildew she had seen! Mildew affected onions do not store as well but are perfectly fine to eat otherwise.

Peppers
Fruit develop on peppers during August. They can be picked as green peppers but outdoor varieties tend to be very bitter tasting when green and are best eaten ripe.

Rocket
Expect the leaves of your rocket to be covered in lots of tiny holes caused by the flea beetle. Although it looks unpleasant, it does not affect the health of the plant (unless very severe) and seems to be pretty much unavoidable (short of growing the crop under tightly pinned down fleece). Your rocket plant may also start to flower. It is best to remove the flowers because the quality of the leaves declines whilst it is in flower.

Sweetcorn
Cobs continue to develop on sweetcorn plants. The cobs will swell and the tassels will turn a chocolate brown colour as they ripen.

Tomatoes
Tomatoes should be continuing to flower and forming fruit throughout August. The first fruits will ripen now, particularly on cherry tomato varieties.

Things to harvest

Basil
Beetroot
Broad beans
Calabrese
Carrots
Celery
Climbing beans
Courgettes
Cucumber
Dwarf beans
Florence fennel
Gherkins
Lettuce
Marjoram
Onions
Parsnips
Potatoes
Rocket
Shallots
Spring onions
Tomatoes
Watercress

Harvesting tips

Basil
Remove individual leaves as and when you require them. It is best to take the newest growth from the tip of the plant. This also helps to prevent it flowering. Although the flowers are very pretty and edible, whilst it is flowering the leaf production dwindles.

Beans
Start picking beans when they are still small and slim. Not only do these young, tender beans taste delicious but also you will soon have a glut so might as well start early. Take care when harvesting the mature beans because there will be immature beans and new flowers further along the same stalk. Hold the stalk with one hand and pull the beans with the other so that you don't pull the whole stalk off – flowers and all. Harvest all the beans that are ready each time and check every 2 to 3 days to encourage new bean formation. If you allow beans to mature then the plant will stop flowering and the crop will stop. If you want to allow some to mature into haricot beans then wait until the end of September to do that.

Lettuce

To harvest a complete lettuce, wait until it has formed a heart then cut it off a ground level. Other lettuce varieties do not form hearts and individual leaves can be removed as and when you require them. If your lettuce plants are growing very close together then thin them out as you harvest them or they will have a tendency to bolt more quickly.

Parsnip

Parsnip grows more slowly than carrot and beetroot sown at the same time so it is only now that it will need thinning; although the germination rate may be so poor that they don't need much thinning. If necessary, thin out by harvesting the slender roots, in the same way as you did for carrots then leave the remainder to develop until after the frosts in October.

Cooking Tips

Aubergines

Aubergines can be used in a number of dishes and are particularly useful to bulk out vegetarian dishes. Before cooking aubergines it is best to slice them, sprinkle them with salt and leave them in the refrigerator for an hour, then dab them dry with kitchen towel. This process removes the bitter taste.

Beans

Using your fingernails, top and tail the beans, then with a sharp knife cut any large ones into lengths of about 1 inch (2.5 cm). Place in a pan of lightly salted water, bring to the boil and simmer for about 5 to 10 minutes until tender. Note that purple beans will turn a dark green on cooking.

Preserving Tips

Freezing

Some people happily freeze their **beans** but I'm not so sure. The beans seem to lose their crispness when frozen. Certainly frozen beans can be used in casseroles etc., and some people would find them totally acceptable to use on their own. I would suggest you try freezing some beans if you have a glut and see what you think. To do so, cut the beans into lengths as you would before cooking them, then blanch them and freeze them (see Equipment and Techniques chapter for more information).

Tomatoes can be frozen for later use in sauces etc. but not for use in salads because the freezing process turns them mushy. This is particularly useful if you are intending to make a recipe requiring a large quantity of tomatoes as they can be frozen as they ripen and stored until you have enough. There is no need to blanch them first.

Pickling
Any very small shallots can be pickled as "pickled onions" (see recipe below).

Drying
Shallots will store well into next year if the foliage has completely died back before lifting and if it is allowed to dry in the sun before being moved to a cool, dry place. At this time of year your cold frame should be empty so you might like to consider stacking them in there temporarily until they dry – move your cold frame into the shade, keep the door open to allow ventilation and make sure that rain can't get in.

In Storage

In the freezer
Broad beans
Calabrese
Fennel
Peas
Soft fruit
Ice cream

In the store cupboard
Pickled beetroot
Chutney
Pickled gherkins
Jam
Jelly
Soup

In cold storage
Garlic

In the kitchen

Pickled Onions

Ingredients
Small shallots

Salt
Malt vinegar

Equipment
Jar and greaseproof paper.

Method
Carefully chop off the shallot roots, trying to retain some of the hard base so that it doesn't fall apart. Peel the shallots (very tedious!). Pack them into a suitable sized jar and cover with heavily salted water (brine). Leave for 24 hours then drain, rinse and dry. Also clean and dry the jar and lid. Repack the shallots in the jar and cover with vinegar. Place a small ball of greaseproof paper in the neck of the jar to keep the shallots submerged.

Storage
Store in a cool dark place for 2 to 3 months before opening then consume within a year before they go soggy.

Usage
As you would normally use pickled onions.

Mixed Salad

There is a huge variety of ingredients that can go into a salad and you will, of course, have your own ideas about the ingredients and the dressing. For this reason I would not like to suggest a recipe for a typical salad, although I have included some recipes for simple salad combinations later on. However, I have provided a list of possible salad ingredients that you might have growing at this time of year.

Ingredients
Lettuce
Cucumber
Tomato
Spring onions
Rocket
Watercress
Basil
Chives
Garlic chives
Beetroot
Carrot

Fennel
Celery
Beans

Tomato and Basil Salad

Ingredients (per serving)
5 to 6 cherry tomatoes
1 tbsp extra virgin olive oil
1 garlic clove
1 small piece of root ginger
1 tsp lime (or lemon) juice
Salt and pepper
1 sprig of basil

Equipment
Small jug or cup, fork, and a serving plate.

Method
Wash the tomatoes and cut into quarters and arrange on a suitable serving plate. Pour the olive oil into a jug. Finely chop the garlic and ginger and add it to the oil. Add the lime juice and seasoning, then whisk the dressing with a fork to make an emulsion. Pour the dressing over the tomatoes, scatter over the torn basil leaves and season to taste. Serve immediately.

Usage
This is a very simple salad that makes excellent use of your first few cherry tomatoes to ripen, or you can make it with slices of larger tomatoes when they are available. It can be served as a starter or as a side dish.

Green Tomato Chutney

Ingredients (makes 3-4 jars)
2lb (900 g) green tomatoes
1lb (450 g) cooking apples
8 oz (225 g) onions
1 oz (25 g) salt
4 oz lb (110 g) sultanas
1 pint (600 ml) malt vinegar
½ tsp ground ginger

1 tbsp pickling spice (e.g. cloves, cinnamon, allspice berries)
8 oz (225 g) light brown sugar
(optional) 1 tbsp black treacle

Equipment
Preserving pan, ladle, jam funnel and 3 to 4 jars.

Method
Plunge the tomatoes into boiling water for a minute or two then rinse them in cold water to remove the skins. Coarsely chop the tomatoes then peel, core and chop the apples (weigh after preparation). Peel and chop the onions and tie the spices in a piece of muslin. Mix all the ingredients except the sugar in the preserving pan and bring to the boil. Drop in the spices. Simmer gently, uncovered, until the pulp is tender (20 to 30 minutes). Add the sugar and stir well until it has completely dissolved. Bring back to the boil and continue to boil until thick. Pour into warm jars and seal immediately.

Storage
Store for 2 months before using, to allow the flavours to develop, then use within a year.

Usage
This is particularly delicious in cheese and chutney sandwiches but also works well as an accompaniment to cold meat.

Red Tomato Chutney

Ingredients (makes 1 jar)
1 lb (450 g) red tomatoes
2 oz (55 g) shallots
2 oz (55 g) caster sugar
¼ oz (7 g) salt
¼ pint (100 ml) malt vinegar
2 to 4 cloves of garlic (depending on size and preference)
Freshly ground black pepper
1 sprig each of rosemary, sage and thyme
2 bay leaves
3 tsp Worcestershire sauce
1 tsp celery salt

Equipment
Preserving pan, cheese grater, ladle, jam funnel and 1 jar.

Method
Plunge the tomatoes into boiling water for about a minute then run under cold water and pinch the skin to remove. Chop them coarsely and add them to the pan. Grate the shallots into the pan and boil the mix for about 10 to 15 minutes. Add the remaining ingredients, stir and simmer until the chutney is thick (see Equipment and Techniques chapter). Remove the bay leaves and pour the hot chutney into a warmed jar and seal immediately.

Storage
Store for 2 months before using, to allow the flavours to develop, then use within a year.

Usage
This makes ideal chutney for sandwiches or as a relish on burgers.

Tomato Sauce for Pasta

Ingredients (1 jar, serves 2)
1 lb (450 g) red tomatoes
4 oz (55 g) shallots or onions
2 cloves of garlic
4 teaspoons of tomato puree
½ tsp salt
½ tsp celery salt
Freshly ground black pepper
1 dessert spoon of olive oil
2 to 3 sprigs of basil

Equipment
Preserving pan, pureeing equipment (see Equipment and Techniques chapter), garlic press, ladle, jam funnel and 1 jar.

Method
Plunge the tomatoes into boiling water for about a minute then run under cold water and pinch the skin to remove. Chop them coarsely and add them to the pan and heat gently until liquefied. Puree the tomatoes (see Equipment and Techniques chapter) and return the liquid to a clean pan. Finely chop or grate the shallots and add them to the pan. Boil for 5 minutes then add the crushed garlic, tomato puree, salt and pepper. Simmer for about 15 minutes then add the olive oil and shredded basil and bring back to the boil. Remove from the heat and transfer into a warmed jar and seal immediately.

Storage
Once the sauce has cooled the safety button should have become depressed again. If it has, then the sauce can be stored for a few months, if not then use within 3 days.

Usage
With pasta as a meal for 2. For example, cook 7 oz (200 g) of pasta as directed on the packet. In the meantime, cut up 2 turkey breasts and stir-fry until cooked through. Drain the pasta, add the meat and the sauce and stir it over a gentle heat until the sauce is hot through. Serve onto 2 plates and sprinkle with grated cheese. Chicken, smoked sausage, pork or bacon can all be substituted for the turkey. This can also be used as lunch by dividing the dish into 3 or 4 portions, transferring them into suitable sized plastic boxes and reheating them in a microwave when required. Any small quantities of the sauce left over can be used as the basis of homemade pizzas (see recipe in November chapter). This sauce is also required in the spinach and ricotta cannelloni and homemade baked bean recipes (November and October chapters respectively).

Tomato and Basil Ketchup

Ingredients (make 6 to 8 bottles)
11 lb (5 kg) tomatoes
1 lb (450 g) onion
2 to 4 garlic cloves
1 lb (450 g) caster sugar
1 pt (500 ml) cider vinegar
2 oz (55 g) salt
2 tbsp tomato puree
2 to 3 tsp soy sauce
Freshly ground black pepper
½ tsp ground all spice
½ tsp paprika
½ tsp ground ginger
3 to 4 sprigs of basil

Equipment
Preserving pan, garlic press, blender/food processor, sieve, ladle, funnel and 6 to 8 bottles.

Method

Wash the tomatoes and add them to the pan. Gently heat, stir and begin to break up the tomatoes. Once the tomatoes have begun to break up, finely chop the onions and add them to the pan. Crush the garlic and add it to the pan then cook the vegetables slowly for about half an hour. In batches, pour the mixture into a blender, liquidise and sieve into a clean bowl. Wash out the pan and return the liquid to it. Add all the other ingredients except the basil, bring to the boil and simmer for several hours until it has reduced to the thickness of ketchup. Add the finely chopped basil, remove from the heat and transfer into warmed bottles and seal immediately.

Storage

Can be stored as for conventional tomato ketchup.

Usage

As you would use conventional tomato ketchup.

Variation

This recipe can also be made with yellow tomato varieties to make "golden" tomato ketchup. Simply substitute the red tomatoes for yellow ones to give unusual golden brown ketchup that tastes the same.

Aubergine, Courgette and Tomato Bake

Ingredients (serves 2)
1 small aubergine or about 5 mini aubergines
Salt and pepper
Oil (for frying)
1 medium onion
1 garlic clove
1 lb (450 g) tomatoes
4 tsp tomato puree
1 handful basil
1 to 2 courgettes (depending on size)
6 oz (170 g) mozzarella
Parmesan

Equipment
2 large frying pans, garlic press, bowl, spatula, ovenproof dish, kitchen towel, and cheese grater.

Method
Slice the aubergine into rounds and sprinkle with salt; cover and place in the refrigerator for about an hour. In the meantime prepare the tomato sauce as follows. Heat the oil in a frying pan, chop the onions finely and fry for 3 to 4 minutes until soft. Add the crushed garlic and stir for another minute then remove from the heat. Drop the tomatoes into boiling water and leave for a minute or two then drain, hold under cold water and pinch the skin to remove it. Chop the tomatoes coarsely and add them to the onions and garlic. Add half the basil, the tomato puree and the seasoning. Bring the mixture to the boil then simmer for 20 to 25 minutes until thick and pulpy; stir occasionally but more frequently towards the end. Preheat the oven to 180 °C, 350 °F, gas mark 4. Grease the ovenproof dish. Remove the aubergine from the refrigerator and pat dry with kitchen towel. In a clean frying pan, fry the aubergines and courgettes until they begin to brown. Spoon half the aubergines and courgettes into the bottom of the dish, cover with half the tomato pulp and place a layer of mozzarella over the top. Spoon over the other half of the aubergines and courgettes and tomato pulp. Shred over the remaining basil and layer it over the mozzarella. Grate the Parmesan over the top and bake for 30 to 40 minutes until the top layer of cheese is golden brown. Serve immediately.

Storage
This dish can be prepared in advance and frozen. It can either be frozen in one dish to serve 2 or as individual portions in smaller dishes. Cook from frozen for 30 to 55 minutes (depending on size) until hot through and golden on top.

Usage
As the basis of a vegetarian meal for 2 with suitable accompaniment.

Vegetable Lasagne

Ingredients (serves 4-6)
For the tomato sauce:
1 medium onion
1-2 cloves of garlic
1 lb (450 g) tomatoes
2 sprigs basil
1 tbsp tomato puree
Salt and pepper
Celery salt

For the mince:
4 oz (110 g) proprietary vegetarian mince (or chicken)
3 rashers vegetarian bacon-style rashers (or smoked bacon back)
6 oz (170 g) mushrooms
6 oz (170 g) aubergine
1 small carrot
1 shallot
1-2 garlic cloves

For the cheese sauce:
2 oz (55 g) butter
2 oz (55 g) plain flour
1 pint (600 ml) milk
4 oz (110 g) grated mature Cheddar cheese
¼ tsp mustard powder

Dried lasagne sheets

Equipment
Frying pan, spatula, food processor, saucepan, wooden spoon, cheese grater, ovenproof dish(es) – e.g. foil containers.

Method
For the tomato sauce:
Finely chop the onion and garlic and fry for 3 to 4 minutes until soft. Plunge the tomatoes in boiling water for a few moments and then run them under cold water to remove the skins. Chop the tomatoes coarsely then add them to the frying pan along with the tomato puree, salt, pepper, celery salt and half the basil. Bring to the boil then simmer until reduced to a thick sauce. Add the remaining basil and stir in.

For the mince:
In the meantime, mince the vegetables (and meat) in a food processor and thoroughly mix. When the tomato sauce is ready add the mince to it and combine well. Then preheat an oven to 180 ° C, 350 °F, gas mark 4.

For the cheese sauce:
Melt the butter in a saucepan then gradually add the flour to it, stirring constantly until it forms a dough ball. Cook for 1 minute then gradually add the milk, stirring continuously so that it does not become lumpy. Simmer for 2 to 3 minutes, whilst stirring, until thick. Add three quarters of the cheese and melt it into the sauce. Add the mustard

powder. In a suitable dish(es), spoon the mince into the bottom, followed by a layer of uncooked pasta, followed by cheese sauce. Continue to layer until all the ingredients are used, finishing with a layer of the cheese sauce. Sprinkle the remaining cheese over the top. Bake for 30 minutes to 1 hour (depending on the size of the dish(es)), until golden brown and cooked through.

Storage
This dish can be made as individual portions and frozen once cooked. Defrost then reheat in the oven at 180 °C, 350 °F, gas mark 4 for 20 minutes until hot through. Alternatively reheat in the microwave. If you are intending to reheat using the microwave, do not prepare the dish in foil containers.

Usage
As a meal for 4 to 6 people.

Steak and Tomato Pie

When I was a child, my favourite food was my granddad's meat pie. I think his secret was adding tomatoes to the filling so this recipe is my attempt to recreate it. I'm sure he used tinned tomatoes but this makes good use of surplus tomatoes.

Ingredients (makes 5 to 6 pies)
1 lb (450 g) lean braising steak, cubed
Oil (for frying)
1 onion
1 garlic clove
2 rashers bacon
6 oz (170 g) vegetables (e.g. mushrooms or carrots)
2 large beef steak tomatoes
1 large sprig of rosemary
2 bay leaves
1 small (25cc) bottle of beer, or stock
3 tsp tomato puree
Salt and pepper
1 oz (25 g) flour
1 block of ready made puff pastry
Milk or egg white to glaze

Equipment
1 frying pan, casserole dish, 5-6 pie cases, rolling pin, bowl, saucepan, slotted spoon, wooden spoon and pastry brush.

Method
Preheat the oven to 180 °C, 350 °F, gas mark 4. Snip the bacon into small pieces and peel and finely chop the onion and garlic. Heat the oil in the frying pan and fry the steak until browned all over. Add the bacon, onion, garlic and vegetable (mushroom or carrot) to the pan and fry until softened. Transfer the contents of the frying pan to the casserole dish. Plunge the tomatoes into boiling water for a few seconds then remove their skins; chop them coarsely and add them to the casserole dish. Season and add the herbs and tomato puree. Stir the ingredients to mix them. Pour the beer into the dish, put the lid on and cook in the oven for 1½ hours. Roll out the pastry and cut around an upturned pie dish to make lids. Once the pie filling is cooked, use a slotted spoon to transfer the meat and vegetables to a bowl. Discard the bay leaves at this point. In a jug or cup, mix the flour with a little cold water to make a thick liquid. Transfer the liquid from the casserole dish into a saucepan and bring to the boil. Just as it reaches the boil, pour the flour/water mix into the pan, stirring continuously as you do so. Boil for a minute or two until the gravy has thickened. Pour the gravy back over the meat and spoon the pie filling equally into the pie cases until they are three-quarters full. Put a pastry lid onto each pie, making a couple of knife marks in each lid as steam vents. Glaze the pastry with milk or egg.

Storage
The pies can be cooked straight away, refrigerated for up to 3 days or frozen until required.

Usage
Cook the thawed pies in a preheated oven at 180 °C, 375 °F, gas mark 5 for 30 to 40 minutes until the pastry has risen and browned. Serve with a suitable accompaniment of potatoes and vegetables.

Broad Bean and Savory Soup

By now your broad beans will be large, have black scars and be tough. This soup is a good way to use up old beans that would otherwise be unpleasant to eat.

Ingredients (makes 1 to 2 jars)
Oil (for frying)
1 medium onion
8 oz (225 g) broad beans (shelled)
1 pint (500 ml) vegetable stock
1 tbsp savory leaves
Salt and pepper

Equipment
Large saucepan or preserving pan, blender/food processor, ladle, funnel and 1 to 2 clean jars.

Method
Shell the broad beans and finely chop the onions. Heat the oil in the bottom of a large saucepan and fry the onion until soft. Add the beans and the stock and bring to the boil. Simmer for 15 to 20 minutes. Add the savory and continue to simmer for a further 2 minutes. Remove the soup from the heat and blend until smooth. Return to a clean saucepan, bring back to the boil, season to taste and add more water if necessary. Serve hot or pour into warmed jars and seal immediately.

Storage
Once the soup has cooled the safety button should have become depressed again. If it has, then the soup can be stored for several months, if not then use within 3 days.

Usage
As a hearty snack with bread.

Borscht (Beetroot Soup)

Ingredients (makes 4 to 5 jars)
6 beetroots weighing a total of about 11 to 11½ oz (300 – 330 g)
Oil (for frying)
1 medium onion
2 carrots
2 garlic cloves
2 tbsp red wine vinegar
2 pints (1100 ml) beef stock (or diluted gravy)
1 floury potato (8 oz; 225 g)
2 bay leaves
Salt and pepper
2 sprig thyme

Equipment
Large saucepan, preserving pan, spatula, blender/food processor, ladle, jam funnel, and 4 to 5 jars.

Method
Twist off the beetroot tops and discard, scrub the beets well to remove all grit. Place the beetroot in a large saucepan, cover with 2 pints (1100 ml) of boiling water and simmer for 30 to 40 minutes until cooked. Remove the beetroot and reserve the cooking water. Peel and dice all of the beetroot but keep one beetroot to one side. Heat the oil in the bottom of the preserving pan and chop the onions. Fry the onions for about 5 minutes until soft. Wash, peel and chop the carrots and crush the garlic. Once the onions are soft add the carrots, garlic and beetroot to the pan and fry for 2 to 3 minutes. Stir in the vinegar and cook for 1 minute whilst stirring. Pour in the beef stock and 1 pint of the beetroot cooking water. Add the peeled and diced potato, bay leaves and seasoning. Bring to the boil then simmer for 45 minutes. Remove the bay leaves and add the thyme and the reserved beetroot. Blend the soup in batches until smooth, then return it to the cleaned pan and reheat, adding seasoning and more water if necessary. Serve hot or ladle into hot jars and seal immediately.

Storage
Once the soup has cooled the safety button should have become depressed again. If it has, then the soup can be stored for several months, if not then use within 3 days.

Usage
This makes a very attractive, fruity soup and its colour and sweetness especially appeals to children. It can be served hot or chilled with bread as a light meal or starter.

Beetroot Cake

Ingredients
10 oz (280 g) grated beetroot (11 oz; 310 g unprepared beetroot)
3 fl oz (85 ml) sunflower oil
4 oz (110 g) caster sugar
3 eggs
6 oz (170 g) flour
3 tsp baking powder
Pinch of salt
1 tsp cinnamon

2 oz (55 g) desiccated coconut

Equipment
Potato peeler, food processor or grater, bowl, round cake tin, wooden spoon, skewer and wire rack.

Method
Preheat an oven to 180 °C, 350 °F, gas mark 4. Wash the beetroot then peel off the skin and cut off the top and tail. Cut the beetroot into quarters and place in a food processor to finely chop, or grate with a cheese grater. Place all the ingredients in a bowl and combine. Grease the cake tin and spoon the cake mix into it. Cook in the centre of the oven for 55 to 60 minutes until golden brown and a skewer inserted into it comes away clean. Allow the cake to cool in the tin for 10 to 20 minutes then turn out onto a wire rack to cool completely.

Storage
Store in an airtight container for up to 3 days.

Usage
As a snack or dessert.

Beetroot and Cucumber Potato Salad

Ingredients (serves 1)
1 medium cooked beetroot
2 inch (5 cm) piece of cucumber
8 oz (225g) waxy potatoes
Cheese

Equipment
Saucepan, cheese grater.

Method
Cook the potatoes in lightly salted water for about 10 minutes until tender. In the meantime, peel and top and tail the beetroot and cut into chunks. Cut the cucumber into chunks too. Once the potatoes are cooked, drain and tip them into a suitable serving dish. Add the cucumber and beetroot chunks and grate cheese over the top.

Usage
This dish can be served immediately as a warm salad dish or allowed to cool and served chilled. It can also be used as a simple packed

lunch if stored in a suitable plastic container. It is a popular salad with children because they generally like both cucumber and beetroot.

Beetroot and Orange Jam

Ingredients (makes 2 to 3 jars)
2 lb (900 g) beetroot
3 oranges
¼ pint (150 ml) lemon juice (freshly squeezed or bottled)
½ tsp ground cinnamon
2 lb (900 g) sugar

Equipment
Saucepan, cheese grater, piece of muslin, preserving pan, wooden spoon, ovenproof dish, ladle, jam funnel, 2 to 3 jars.

Method
Boil the beetroot for the appropriate amount of time (see June) and allow it to cool. Remove their skins, top and tail and cut into small chunks. Put the beetroot chunks into the preserving pan. Cut one of the oranges in half then grate the zest from one half of the orange and add it to the pan. Squeeze the juice from the same half of orange and add that to the pan. Peel the remaining half and other two oranges, retaining the peel. Chop the oranges into small chunks and set aside. Place the peel, pith and any pips into a piece of muslin, tie the piece of muslin into a bundle and add it to the pan; also add the lemon juice to the pan. Sprinkle the cinnamon into the pan too. Bring the contents of the pan to the boil and simmer for 20-30 minutes. Stir occasionally throughout this time but check more frequently towards the end and stop cooking when there is no more visible liquid. Remove the muslin bundle. Now add the sugar; stir it in then leave the mixture for about 10 minutes. After this time, liquid should have been extracted from the beetroot and it should be possible to stir the mixture until the sugar is completely dissolved. Gentle heating may help the sugar dissolve. Add the orange segments and bring the mixture to the boil. Boil rapidly for 5 to 10 minutes until the setting point is reached. In the meantime heat some jars in a cool oven. Once the setting point is reached, remove the jam from the heat and allow it to cool for 5 minutes before transferring to jars and sealing.

Storage
Store in a cool, dark place for up to 2 years. Once opened keep in the refrigerator.

Usage
This is a very unusual jam and it retains both the earthy flavour of the beetroot and the citrus tang of the oranges, as well as being sweet. It is best used as you might use chutney, i.e. with cold meat and cheese.

Cucumber Chutney

Ingredients (makes 1 jar)
For every 1 lb cucumbers:
8 oz (225 g) apples
1 large onion (8 oz; 225 g)
1 to 2 sticks of celery (depending on size)
½ pint (300 ml) white wine vinegar
8 oz (225 g) light brown sugar
1 tbsp salt
¼ tsp turmeric
Pinch of ground allspice (Jamaican pepper)
2 tsp balsamic vinegar

Equipment
Food processor, non-metallic bowl, small plate, preserving pan, wooden spoon, ladle, jam funnel and 1 jar per lb of cucumber.

Method
Cube but don't peel the cucumber then finely slice it in a food processor. Peel the onion and core, but don't peel, the apples. Use the food processor to finely chop the celery sticks, apple and the onion. Place the vegetables in the bowl and place a small plate on top. Press down on the plate to squeeze the water out of the vegetables, and discard. Place the vegetables in the preserving pan and cook for about 10 minutes, stirring to avoid sticking. Pour in the vinegar, sugar and other flavourings and bring to the boil. Simmer, stirring occasionally until the liquid has almost gone. Ladle into a warmed jar and seal immediately.

Storage
Leave for 1 month for the flavours to develop before opening and consume within a year.

Usage
To accompany salads, cheese or cold meat or in sandwiches.

Subsequent Years

Thing to expect

Fruit
The top leaves of **currant** bushes may become distorted due to aphids. This generally doesn't cause any problems and can be ignored. **Plums** will become ripe some time during August depending on the variety and the weather. **Apples** should also ripen during this month.

Things to harvest
Apples
Plums

Harvesting Technique

Plums
As each variety of plums varies considerably in its colour when ripe, it is difficult to suggest a colour to look out for to check ripeness. However, you will quickly get used to the colour of your variety of plums. If you are intending to eat the plums or use them in puddings then wait until they are fully ripe before picking. They should be soft and springy to the touch and when very ripe they will fall from the tree. When cut open the stone will come away from the flesh easily. If you intend to make jam then the plums should be picked when just ripe or slightly under ripe. The plums will still have some firmness to them and possibly a vague hint of green at this stage and when cut the stone is difficult to remove. Unfortunately, wasps also like plums so look out for these when harvesting.

In the kitchen

Apple and Cinnamon Rolls

Ingredients (makes 10)
2 apples
1 block of ready-made puff pastry
2 oz (55 g) caster sugar
2 tsp ground cinnamon
Egg white
Brown sugar

Equipment
Bowl, rolling pin, baking tray, pastry brush and wire rack.

Method
Preheat an oven to 220 °C, 425 °F, gas mark 7. Peel, core and dice the apples then toss them in the caster sugar and cinnamon until well coated. Roll the pastry out to a rectangle about 15 by 12 inches (38 by 30 cm). Cut the pastry in half lengthways. Spoon half the spiced apple mixture down the long sides of each pastry piece. Brush the long end of each pastry piece with egg white. Fold the pastry over as if making a sausage roll and seal, using the egg white as "glue". Cut each roll diagonally into 5 pieces and place on a baking tray, with the fold facing downward. Glaze with egg white and sprinkle with brown sugar. Cook for 15 minutes, remove from the tray immediately and cool on a wire rack.

Storage
Best served soon after cooking but can be eaten the next day too.

Usage
As a snack or dessert either served on its own or with cream.

Variation
This recipe can also be made by substituting the fresh apples, caster sugar and cinnamon with apple and ginger jam (see recipe below).

Apple and Cinnamon Sandwich Crumble

Ingredients (serves 4)
2½ oz (70 g) self-raising flour
3 oz (85 g) oats
3½ oz (100 g) soft dark brown sugar
½ tsp salt
3 oz (85 g) margarine
2 medium apples

Equipment
Bowl and loaf tin.

Method
Preheat an oven to 190 °C, 375 °F, gas mark 5. Melt the margarine then combine it with all the other ingredients apart from the apples and mix until crumbly. Spoon half the mixture into the bottom of a greased

loaf tin and press down. Peel and slice the apples then layer them onto the mixture in the tin. Cover with the remaining mixture and press down lightly. Cook for 30 to 40 minutes. Serve immediately.

Storage
This dish is best served straight from the oven but can be cooled, refrigerated overnight and reheated the next day.

Usage
Serve hot with custard as a dessert.

Spiced Apple Crumble

Ingredients (serves 4 to 6)
For the filling:
2 lb (900 g) apples
1 oz soft dark brown sugar
2 cloves
1 tsp cinnamon
3 oz (85g) raisins
2 tbsp water

For the crumble:
4 oz (110 g) wholemeal flour
4 oz (110 g) oats
3 oz (85 g) butter
5 oz (140g) soft dark brown sugar

Equipment
Bowl and ovenproof dish.

Method
Preheat an oven to 180 °C, 350 °F, gas mark 4. Place the flour, oats and baking powder in a bowl. Chop up the butter and add it to the dry ingredients. Rub the butter in with your fingertips until the mixture is crumbly and resembles breadcrumbs. Add the sugar and combine. Peel, core and slice the apples. Place the apples, raisins, sugar and spices in a saucepan with the water and cook gently for a few minutes until the apples are soft and fluffy. Spoon the fruit into a suitable dish. Sprinkle the crumble mix over the fruit and spread out evenly. Bake on a high shelf in the oven for 30 to 40 minutes until the topping is slightly brown. Serve immediately.

Storage
This dish is best served immediately although it can be stored overnight in the refrigerator then reheated the next day. It can be made in advance and frozen. However, it is more economical on freezer space to cook the fruit filling, freeze it separately, then defrost and use in this recipe.

Usage
Serve hot with cream or custard as a filling dessert.

Apple and Ginger Jam

Ingredients (makes 5 to 7 jars)
3 lb (1400 g) apples
16½ fl oz (450 ml) water
3 lb 6 oz (1570 g) sugar
6 oz (170 g) stem ginger
3 tbsp stem ginger syrup

NB: Every pound of apples requires 1 lb 2 oz sugar, 5½ fl oz water, 2 oz stem ginger and 1 tbsp ginger syrup.

Equipment
Preserving pan, wooden spoon, ovenproof dish, ladle, jam funnel and 5 to 7 jars.

Method
Peel, cut the apples into quarters and core. Place in a preserving pan with the water and bring slowly to the boil. Simmer the apples for about 10 minutes until they are soft and pulpy. In the meantime warm the sugar and cut the stem ginger into small pieces. Once the fruit is cooked add the sugar, ginger and the syrup to the fruit and stir over a low heat until all the sugar is dissolved. Boil rapidly for 5 to 8 minutes until the setting point in reached. Ladle into warmed jars and seal immediately.

Storage
For up to 2 years in a cool, dry place. Store in the refrigerator once opened.

Usage
Although this is a very tasty jam that is delicious used simply on toast, it is worth making in order to use as an ingredient for other recipes.

These include apple and cinnamon rolls (see recipe above), apple and apricot flapjacks and apple, oat and raisin muffins (see recipes below).

Apple and Apricot Flapjacks

Ingredients (makes 12)
4¾ oz (135 g) margarine
5¼ oz (150 g) apple and ginger jam
8 oz (225 g) oats
Pinch of salt
¾ oz (20 g) sunflower seeds
1¾ oz (50 g) dried apricots

Equipment
9-inch (23-cm) square cake tin, large saucepan, wooden spoon.

Method
Preheat an oven to 190 °C, 375 °F, gas mark 5. Line and grease the cake tin. In a large saucepan, gently melt together the margarine and the jam. Remove from the heat and add oats, salt, seeds and chopped apricots. Stir well until fully combined. Spoon into the cake tin and press well down with wetted fingers. Bake for 15 to 20 minutes until golden brown. Mark out to 12 pieces then allow it to cool completely in the tin.

Storage
Store in an airtight container for up to a week.

Usage
As a filling, nutritious snack.

Apple, Oat and Raisin Muffins

Ingredients (makes 8)
6 oz (170 g) oats
4 oz (110 g) plain flour
1 oz (25 g) light muscovado sugar
2 oz (55g) raisins
1 tsp baking powder
½ tsp bicarbonate of soda
½ tsp ground cinnamon
Pinch of salt

2½ tbsp apple and ginger jam
3 fl oz (85 ml) apple juice
1 egg
2 tbsp sunflower oil
1 tbsp skimmed milk

Equipment
Large bowl, small bowl, fork, muffin tin, muffin cases and wire rack,

Method
Preheat an oven to 200 °C, 400 °F, gas mark 6. Grease a muffin tin and line with 8 paper cases. Combine all the dry ingredients in a large bowl. Combine all the wet ingredients in a small bowl. Add the wet mix to the dry mix and stir together with a fork until it is just mixed. Spoon the mixture into 8 muffin cases so that each case is three quarters full. If your muffin tin has more than 8 spaces, pour a small amount of water into each empty space to allow for more even cooking. Bake in the oven for 20 to 22 minutes until well-risen and golden brown. Allow the muffins to cool for 5 minutes in the tin before transferring onto a wire rack to cool completely.

Storage
Store in an airtight container for up to 5 days.

Usage
As a snack or dessert.

Apple and Sage Cheese

Cheeses are different again from jam and jellies but much of the technique is the same. Pleased read the jam and jelly making section in the Equipment and Techniques chapter if you haven't already done so.

Ingredients (makes 4 to 6 jars)
3 lb (1400 g) apples
Sugar
4 tbsp chopped fresh sage leaves

Equipment
Preserving pan, jelly bag or alternative (see Equipment and Techniques chapter), bowl, wooden spoon, ladle, jam funnel and 4 to 6 jars.

Method

Wash and chop the apples. Place the apples in a preserving pan and cook for 20 to 30 minutes until the fruit is very soft and pulp. Strain the pulp through a jelly bag overnight over a bowl (see Equipment and Techniques chapter). The clear juice is not required in this recipe but can be used to make jelly (see recipe below). Squeeze the pulp through the jelly bag or a fine sieve or piece of muslin. Weigh the pulp and weigh out 1 lb (450 g) of sugar for every 1 lb (450 g) of pulp. Transfer the pulp and the sugar to a preserving pan and bring slowly to the boil, stirring continuously until the sugar is dissolved. Continue to boil until the mixture is so thick that a clean line is left when you draw a spoon across the bottom of the pan. Add the sage leaves, stir in and remove from the heat. Transfer into warmed jars and seal immediately.

Storage

Can be stored in a cool dry place for up to 2 years. Once opened, store in the refrigerator and use up quickly.

Usage

Although this is fairly sweet, it is designed to go with savoury dishes such as meat. Is ideally suited as an accompaniment to pork or game. It can be used as a substitute for conventional applesauce. It also adds a pleasant flavour when included in stuffing for chicken or as a glaze on roast pork (see recipe). Below are 3 recipes for pork using this cheese.

Pork and Apple Burgers

Ingredients (makes 5-6)
14 oz (400g) minced pork
1 small onion or 1 large shallot
1 garlic clove (optional)
2 slices of bread (crumbled)
Salt and pepper
A few sage leaves
3½ oz (100 g) apple and sage cheese (or use finely chopped fresh apples)
1 egg
Flour

Equipment
Bowl, food processor, chopping board, pastry cutter, cling film, palette knife, fish slice.

Method

Tip the mince into a bowl and separate. Chop the onion, garlic and sage in a food processor and add to the mince. Season with salt and pepper. Rub 2 slices of bread to make breadcrumbs and add this to the mix. Add the apple and sage cheese and egg and mix in. Flour a chopping board or plate. Press the meat mixture into the pastry cutter until it is about ½ inch (1.3 cm) deep. Transfer the burger onto cling film using a palette knife or fish slice, then repeat until all the mixture is used. Either refrigerate or freeze in pairs. Cook from thawed for about 12-15 minutes.

Storage
Can be refrigerated for up to 3 days or frozen.

Usage
These can be served as part of a meal or cooked with burger buns for a light meal. To cook with a burger bun try the following. Line a grill pan with foil and grill 2 burgers for 12 to 15 minutes, turning once. Set the burgers to one side and remove the foil from the grill pan. Slice 2 burger buns in half and grill both halves. Set the lids of the buns to one side. Place the burger on the bottom half of the bun, smear the top of the burger with mustard and place a dollop of ketchup on each. Sprinkle over a small amount of diced, raw onion or shallot, add a slice of pickled gherkin and a slice of cheese. Return the burger to the grill to melt the cheese. Add some fresh tomato and lettuce and place the lid of the burger bun on the top. Serve immediately.

Roast Pork Glazed with Apple and Sage Cheese

Ingredients
Pork joint
Salt
Apple and sage cheese

Equipment
Kitchen towel, roasting tin

Method

Preheat an oven to 180 °C, 350 °F, gas mark 4. Make sure that the skin on the pork is well scored then pat it dry with kitchen towel, rub salt into it and, after a few minutes, pat it dry again. Then smear generous amounts of apple and sage cheese over the exposed meat of the joint and place it in a roasting tin. Ideally, the apple and sage cheese should only be cooked on the meat for about an hour to an hour and a half. If you have a particularly large piece of meat that requires a longer cooking time, cover the joint over with foil until an hour and a half before it is ready. Once cooked, allow the meat to rest for 10 minutes before carving.

Usage

Serve as part of a roast dinner. The meat will have a subtle sweet, apple flavour to it but if you prefer a stronger flavour, serve the meat with a few spoonfuls of uncooked apple and sage cheese.

Mustard Pork Hotpot

This "hotpot" is "hot" both in temperature and flavour. The combination of the mustard and the apple and sage cheese gives this dish both a sweet and hot flavour that is unusual but appealing. Because the ingredients are also available later in the year, this is a good dish to make as a winter warmer.

Ingredients (serves 2 to 4)
Oil for frying
Potatoes
Salt and pepper
2 to 4 pork chops
1 red onion
1 medium carrot
1 pint (600 ml) stock (chicken or vegetable)
3 tsp sage mustard (ordinary mustard will do)
2 tbsp apple and sage cheese
Celery salt

Equipment

Frying pan, tongs, spatula, casserole dish (without lid), and 2 saucepans.

Method

Preheat an oven to 190 °C, 375 °F, gas mark 5. Wash, peel and cut the potatoes into rounds. Par boil them, drain and allow them to cool enough to be handled. Heat the oil in the frying pan and season the pork chops. Fry the pork for 1 to 2 minutes on each side until just browned then place it in the bottom of a casserole dish. Smear mustard over one surface of each chop. Cut the onion into wedges and fry until beginning to brown then add it to the casserole dish. Peel the carrot and cut into rounds; stir fry it for 2 to 3 minutes then add it to the casserole dish. In the meantime, heat the stock and the cheese in a saucepan until just beginning to boil. Pour the stock over the meat and vegetables. Arrange the potato over the dish so that it forms a layer. Season with celery salt then place the dish in the oven for 50 minutes to 1 hour until cooked through and the potatoes are golden brown and crispy. Serve immediately.

Usage

As a complete meal for 2 to 4 people.

Sweet Pork and Apple Casserole

This is similar to the previous recipe but has a sweeter flavour with less of a bite. If you have apples that store well then this recipe can also be made later in the year as a winter warmer.

Ingredients (serves 2)

Oil for frying
Potatoes
Salt and pepper
2 pork chops
2 rashers of bacon
2 gloves of garlic
1 large cooking apple
1 onion
1 medium carrot
¼ pint (150 ml) cider or apple juice

Equipment

Frying pan, tongs, spatula, casserole dish (with lid).

Method

Preheat an oven to 140 °C, 275 °F, gas mark 1. Heat the oil in the frying pan and season the pork chops. Fry the pork for 1 to 2 minutes on each side until just browned then place in the bottom of a casserole dish. Add the bacon to the frying pan and fry until the fat begins to run. Place a rasher on top of each chop. Peel the garlic and cut into thin slices and arrange on top of the bacon. Peel, core and cut the apple into small slices and arrange on top of the bacon. Peel and finely cut the onion and the carrot, and arrange them around the chops. Pour the cider or juice into the dish. Wash, peel and cut the potatoes into rounds. Arrange the potato over the dish so that it forms a layer. Use an oil sprayer (if you have one) or a brush to cover the potatoes in a thin film of oil. Season with salt and pepper. Place the lid on the dish and put it into the oven for 3 hours. Then remove the lid and place the dish under the grill to crisp the top of the potatoes.

Usage
As a complete meal for 2.

Apple and Rosemary Jelly

This can be made either as a separate recipe or to make use of the juice not required for the apple and sage cheese recipe above.

Ingredients (makes 3 to 4 jars)
Reserved juice from the apple and sage cheese recipe (see above)
Sugar
5 sprigs of rosemary

Equipment
Preserving pan, wooden spoon, jelly bag (or alternative), bowl, ovenproof dish, ladle, jam funnel, 3 to 4 jars.

Method
Measure the strained liquid and weigh 1 lb sugar for every pint of liquid collected. Pour the liquid into a clean preserving pan and stir in the rosemary leaves and the warmed sugar. Stir over a low heat until the sugar has completely dissolved then bring to the boil and heat rapidly for 3 to 5 minutes until the setting point is reached. Ladle into hot jars and seal immediately.

Storage
Store in a cool, dry place for up to 2 years.

Usage
This is a very attractive jelly. It can be used as an accompaniment to meats such as beef and lamb.

Plum Jam

Please read the jelly making section of the Equipment and Techniques chapter before making this recipe if you haven't already done so. This recipe is best made with slightly under ripe plums as it tends to set better.

Ingredients (makes 4 to 5 jars)
3 lb (1400 g) plums
¼ pint (150 ml) water
3 lb (1400 g) sugar

NB: Every pound of plums requires 1¾ fl oz (50 ml) water and 1 pound (450 g) sugar.

Equipment
Preserving pan, wooden spoon, ovenproof dish, ladle, jam funnel, 4 to 5 jars.

Method
Wash the plums, cut in half and remove the stone. Put the plums in a preserving pan with the water and cook for 20 to 30 minutes until soft and pulpy. In the meantime warm the sugar. Once the fruit is cooked, add the warm sugar and stir over a gentle heat until completely dissolved. Bring to the boil and heat rapidly for 10 to 15 minutes until the setting point is reached. This jam has a tendency to stick to the bottom of the pan and burn. Usually, stirring during the vigorous boiling stage is not recommended as it can cause the rolling boil to be lost. However, it is worth a quick stir now and then to check that the bottom is clear and a more thorough stir if fruit or sugar is sticking to the bottom. Try not to lose the rolling boil when stirring as this may affect its setting ability but this is probably better than having the jam tainted with burnt sugar. Skim off any scum then ladle into jars and seal immediately.

Storage
Store in a cool, dry place for up to 2 years.

Usage
This is a very popular jam simply for use on toast but can be used in cakes and tarts too.

Variation
Plum and cinnamon jam can be made by adding a cinnamon stick whilst cooking the fruit. Remove the stick before adding the sugar with 1 to 2 teaspoons of ground cinnamon to taste.

Plum and Mulled Wine Jam

Please read the jelly making section of the Equipment and Techniques chapter before making this recipe if you haven't already done so. This recipe is best made with slightly under ripe plums as it tends to set better.

Ingredients (makes 5 to 6 jars)
4 lb (1800 g) plums
½ bottle (360 ml) cheap red wine (or expensive if you're going to drink the other half!)
1 cinnamon stick
½ nutmeg
2 tsp cloves
4 lb (1800 g) sugar

Equipment
Preserving pan, piece of muslin, wooden spoon, ovenproof dish, ladle, jam funnel, 4 to 5 jars.

Method
Wash the plums, cut in half and remove the stone. Put the plums in a preserving pan with the wine. Tie the spices into a bundle of muslin and add it to the pan. Cook for 20 to 30 minutes until soft and pulpy. In the meantime warm the sugar. Once the fruit is cooked, remove the muslin bundle and add the warm sugar and stir over a gentle heat until completely dissolved. Bring to the boil and heat rapidly for 10 to 15 minutes until the setting point is reached. Ladle into jars and seal immediately.

Storage
Store in a cool, dry place for up to 2 years.

Usage

Can be used as you would for any jam. It has a full, festive flavour so is a good one to get out for Christmas. Be reassured that by the time the jam is cooked there is little or no alcohol remaining (not that you'll care if you drank the other half bottle while making the jam!).

Plum and Orange Mincemeat

Ingredients (makes 5 to 6 jars)
3 lb (1400 g) plums
1 lb (450 g) mixed dried fruit
2 large oranges
3 lb (1400 g) sugar
2 cinnamon sticks

Equipment

Non-metallic bowl, preserving pan, wooden spoon, ovenproof dish, ladle, jam funnel, 5 to 6 jars.

Method

Wash the plums, cut in half, remove the stones and chop into pieces. Place the plums in a non-metallic bowl and add the dried fruit. Peel the oranges and chop into small pieces and add to the bowl with the other fruit. Pour the sugar into the bowl and stir well until all the fruit is coated. Cover and leave for a few hours or overnight. Pour the mix into the preserving pan, add the cinnamon sticks and heat gently until the sugar is thoroughly dissolved. Bring it to the boil and then simmer for about half an hour until the mixture is thick. Remove the cinnamon sticks and pour into warmed jars and seal immediately.

Storage

Store in a cool, dry place for up to 2 years.

Usage

This recipe has a fruity, festive flavour so is a good one to get out for Christmas. It can be used to make an alternative to conventional mince pies or as a fruity accompaniment to other desserts, or dollopped into your porridge.

September

For some people, September seems like the end of the season and you may be expecting your crops to dwindle and the work on the plot to be over. However, until the first frosts arrive you can expect to harvest a good number of crops. And as the frosts don't tend to arrive until October or later (unless you are in Scotland), you can expect to be harvesting for all of this month, sometimes willing things to ripen just in time before the weather kills them off. As the weather will turn and the harvests dwindle during October, September is an important month for storing and preserving food for the winter.

Every year

Things to do

Beans
Keep harvesting regularly to encourage a continuous crop. Wait until mid-September before allowing some of your climbing beans to develop into haricots.

Onions
By now the foliage on the onions should have died back. If not, bend the leaves over at the top of the bulb to encourage them to die back. Once the foliage is dry, lift all the onions. This should be done on a dry day and the bulbs allowed to dry in the sun before being stored. They can be stored in shallow boxes, tied into strings or plaited. You may like to temporarily store them in your cold frame whilst they dry but make sure your cold frame is in the shade and that you leave the door open on warm days and closed if raining.

Potatoes
Continue to remove any blighted potato plants. All main crop potatoes should be lifted during this month or next. This is best done on a warm, dry day and the tubers should be allowed to dry in the sun for their skins to set. Store temporarily in shallow boxes whilst they dry, turning occasionally, then transfer to potato sacks for more permanent storage. Remove any damaged potatoes and discard or use these first because they won't store well and could turn others bad too. Make sure that you store the potatoes in the dark because they will quickly turn green and later will develop sprouts sooner if they are in the light. The storage place needs to be frost-free because potatoes will go soggy and mouldy if they freeze and thaw.

Pumpkins and melons
Protect the underside of any developing fruit to prevent soil, stones or slugs damaging the fruit. Simply place a piece of glass, plastic, wood or similar underneath each fruit.

Soil
As soil becomes vacant, cover it with opaque plastic, cardboard or carpet to prevent weeds growing. This will greatly help you in the following spring when you will not need to weed and dig over your beds.

Tomatoes
Continue to spray tomatoes fortnightly with copper fungicide to protect from blight. Continue to feed fortnightly too.

Things to expect

Autumn crops
By now your autumn crops should all have germinated and be growing away well. Their growth rate will slow down as the weather cools.

Beans
You may find your climbing beans are attacked by blackfly, helped by their own personal army of ants. It is possible to control, or at least slow down, an attack by removing the affected leaves. However, if it is very severe you may consider spraying them.

Broccoli
Caterpillars may be rampant on your broccoli by now; continue to remove and squash by hand or resort to spraying if necessary.

Cape gooseberries
If cape gooseberries are going to produce a useful crop before the frosts then they should be producing fruit by now. These are contained within Chinese lantern type husks. When they are almost ripe the husks fall to the ground and the fruit continues to ripen there.

Cucurbits
If you hadn't already noticed, your cucurbits will probably have developed mildew by now. This looks like a white powder all over the leaves. It doesn't seem to particularly affect the harvest and no action is necessary. It can be controlled with the same copper-based fungicide used for blight.

Potatoes

Expect more damage on your main crop potatoes than you found on your first and second early crops. Discard any blight-blackened tubers. You may also find more slug holes. These potatoes won't store well but can be eaten by cutting out the damaged parts. You may find some rough patches on the surface caused by scab. These are fine to store and are perfectly acceptable to eat, particularly if peeled first.

Things to harvest

Aubergines
Basil
Beetroot
Calabrese
Cape gooseberries
Carrot
Celery
Climbing beans
Courgette
Cucumbers
Florence fennel
Gherkins
Lettuce
Melons
Onions
Peppers
Potatoes
Pumpkins
Red cabbage
Rocket
Spring onions
Sweetcorn
Tomatoes

Harvesting Tips

Celery

Celery can either be harvested as a whole plant or individual stems can be removed as required. Either way, cut them free with a sharp knife.

Peppers

Peppers will stop producing fruit if they are allowed to ripen. However, as the end of the season approaches it is worth while allowing peppers to change colour and ripen. To harvest, use a sharp knife to cut through the stem holding on the fruit.

Pumpkins and melons
To harvest pumpkins and melons, wait until the fruit is totally ripe, then cut the stem with a sharp knife.

Red cabbage
This is ready to pick once it has formed a heart and looks like a firm ball. Simply slice through the base of the cabbage with a sharp knife. Remove any outer leaves whilst still outside because they can harbour earwigs, woodlice, slugs and snails.

Sweetcorn
Judging when sweetcorn is ready to harvest has to be one of the most difficult things to do. The first clue is that the tassels have turned a dark chocolate brown colour. When you feel the cob, it should be a good size and firm. You can try gently prising apart the surrounding greenery until you expose the cob itself. If it is ripe you should see some good-sized kernels (although the very tip rarely develops probably so don't be misled). They should have at least a hint of yellow to them and should ooze a milky liquid when burst with a fingernail. My paranoia is that I will miss the time when the sweetcorn is perfectly ripe because this feels like such a short period. It seems that they quickly become over ripe with dark yellow kernels and a very cloudy, starchy liquid. When sweetcorn are perfectly ripe they are the most delicious crop you will ever taste so it is worth a gamble. I always harvest my first few when they are slightly under ripe. They are still edible, although a little bland, but I'd rather that than miss the crucial time. If you think the cob is still under ripe, try to pull the greenery back round it, although it will never go back perfectly and earwigs will probably decide it makes a nice home – they won't damage the cob but it might give you a fright next time! If you think it is ripe, grasp the cob firmly and yank it downward to remove it from the plant. It should come away with some greenery and possibly the nearest leaf too. It is worth removing some of this foliage whilst still outside because earwigs like to live in amongst it and you don't want them in your kitchen. Leave some greenery on to protect it on the way back to the kitchen. Sweetcorn starts to convert its glucose (sugar) to starch from the moment it is picked so you should try to eat it, or freeze it, as soon as possible after picking.

Cooking Tips

Sweetcorn

Remove all the outer foliage and pull away the silks. If the sweetcorn is ripe it should be slightly yellow (depending on the variety) and will become a darker yellow on cooking. If the cobs are very long they may need cutting in half with a large, sharp knife to fit into the pan. Cut the cob all round until you meet resistance then snap it in half. Place them in a pan of unsalted boiling water. Boil for 10 minutes, drain and serve. Salting the water makes the kernels tough but salt can be added at the table. Serve simply with salt and butter or olive oil and black pepper. Corn on the cob is delicious as a side dish or a starter.

Preserving Tips

Freezing

Sweetcorn freezes very well. You may have some cobs with only a few kernels dotted around it due to poor pollination. For these, take a sharp knife and cut off the kernels to make loose sweetcorn. If, however, the cob is complete then freeze it whole and eat it as corn on the cob. You may wish to trim off the end to make it smaller and neater. The corn should be blanched before freezing (see Equipment and Techniques chapter for more details) and frozen as soon as possible after it is picked.

Peppers (both capsicums and chilli) can also be frozen for later use on pizzas or in other cooked dishes. Cut the peppers, remove the seeds and chop into small pieces. Then blanch and freeze (see Equipment and Techniques chapter for more details).

Most **herbs** can be frozen. To do so, remove any stems and place the leaves in bags and freeze. Once frozen, scrunch the bag to break the herbs into pieces. Use from frozen. Alternatively, place small quantities of cut herbs into an ice-cube tray, fill with water and freeze. To use, add the whole ice cube to the dish you are cooking.

Pickling
Red cabbage can be pickled very successfully (see recipe below).

Drying

Onions will store well into next year if the foliage has completely died back before lifting and if it is allowed to dry in the sun before being moved to a cool, dry place. At this time of year your cold frame should be empty so you might like to consider stacking them in there at least temporarily until they dry – just remember to keep the door open to allow ventilation and make sure that rain can't get in. Ultimately the cold frame will be too warm (and later, too cold) for long term storage and the bulbs should be removed to somewhere cool and dry.

Chilli peppers dry successfully. To do this, hang them up whole in a warm dry place (such as an airing cupboard and they will gradually begin to dry and shrivel.

Herbs are preserved well by drying them. You may find that you have large enough evergreen herbs that you can continue to harvest fresh herbs throughout the year. However, if your herb plants are still small they may not tolerate defoliating throughout the winter so you should preserve some now. Also, if your herbs are not close to your house, you may want a supply of easily accessible dried herbs to see you through the winter. Some herbs, such as basil, will be killed by the first frosts and need preserving now. To dry herbs, remove them in sprigs, tie them up in bunches and hang them up in a warm, dry place (such as an airing cupboard) to dry. Alternatively, pick individual leaves and place them in a single layer on a tray in the airing cupboard. After about a fortnight they should be crisp to the touch and crumble between your fingers. Strip them from their stems and crumble them into suitable jars and label. Dried herbs retain their flavour longer if stored in the dark. To dry herbs more quickly, place them in a single layer on a baking tray and put them in a cool oven (e.g. 50 °C) with the door open for about half an hour to an hour until crisp. It is very important to keep the oven door open or you will cook rather than dry your herbs. I would recommend drying and storing some herbs separately so that you can be selective about the flavours you include in a recipe. However, I would also recommend combining some herbs in specific mixes (see recipes below). September is another good time to make another batch of herb mustards so look back at the recipes given in May.

Cool storage
Pumpkins, melons, and potatoes will store well if keep in a cool, frost free and dry environment. They should keep at least until Christmas time like this, although it is worth checking them regularly to check for signs of rot.

In Storage

In the freezer
Broad beans
Calabrese
Climbing beans (possibly)
Fennel
Peas
Strawberries
Tomatoes
Ice cream

In the store cupboard
Pickled beetroot
Borscht
Broad bean soup
Chutney
Pickled cucumber
Pickled gherkins
Jam
Jelly
Pickled onions
Pea and bacon soup
Tomato sauce
Tomato ketchup

In cold storage
Garlic
Shallots

In the kitchen

Pickled Cabbage

Ingredients
1 red cabbage
Salt
Malt vinegar

Equipment
Jars, non-metallic bowl, small plate and greaseproof paper.

Method

Remove any damaged outer leaves and wash the cabbage. Use a large, serrated knife to cut the cabbage into strips. Remove and discard any thick and tough stems and veins. Layer the cabbage into a non-metallic bowl with salt. Place a small plate on top of the cabbage and weight it down. Leave for several hours or overnight. Drain off any water, wash the cabbage under a cold tap and dry. Pack well into suitable sized jars then fill with vinegar. Place a ball of greaseproof paper into the neck of the jar to keep the cabbage submerged and seal the jar.

Storage

Store in a cool, dry place a month before opening. Consume within a year before the cabbage goes soft.

Usage

As an accompaniment to cold meats or in stir-fries (see recipe below)

Sweet and Sour Chicken and Rice

Ingredients (serves 2)
6½ oz (180g) brown rice (or 7 oz, 200 g of white)
1 skinless chicken breast
Oil (for frying)
2 pineapple rings
1 tbsp frozen peas
1 tbsp loose sweetcorn (fresh or frozen)
1 small carrot
1½ inch (4 cm) piece of cucumber
1 tbsp pickled cabbage
Salt and pepper
1 packet of sweet and sour sauce (of your choosing)

Equipment

Saucepan, frying pan (or wok) and sieve.

Method

Boil some water and put the rice on to cook. In the meantime, cut the chicken breast into small pieces. Heat the oil in a frying pan (or wok) and fry the chicken for 8 to 10 minutes until cooked through and browned. Cut the cucumber and carrots into julienne and cut the pineapple into pieces then stir-fry with the other vegetables and the chicken for 2 to 3 minutes until cooked but still crunchy. Add the sauce to the pan and heat through. Serve immediately with the rice.

Usage
As a meal for 2. The combination of vegetables in this recipe may seem a little odd but somehow pickled red cabbage and slightly cooked cucumber seem to work well together. It can be quite a popular stir-fry for children as it contains the types of vegetables they tend to like. This recipe can also be prepared in advance and reheated in the microwave for lunch. To do this, cook the rice, drain and rinse with cold water. Grill the chicken for 15 minutes then cool and cut into pieces. Place the rice and meat in a bowl and add the uncooked vegetables and sauce. Stir well to combine. Divide it into 3 servings of approximately 7 oz (200 g) each and store in suitable plastic containers. They can be stored in the refrigerator for up to 3 days and reheated in the microwave for approximately 2 minutes as a filling and nutritious lunch. To use as a prepared dinner, divide into 2 portions of approximately 12½ oz (350 g) each and reheat as required.

Chicken Casserole with Shallots and Courgette

Ingredients
Oil (for frying)
2 skinless chicken breasts
Freshly ground black pepper
4 rashers smoked back bacon
1 to 2 garlic cloves (depending on size and preference)
½ pint (300 ml) red or rosé wine
1 bay leaf
6 to 8 small shallots (weighing about 4 oz, 110 g)
1 courgette

Equipment
Frying pan, spatula, casserole dish and lid, and a small saucepan.

Method
Preheat an oven to 180 °C, 350 °F, gas mark 4. Heat the oil in the frying pan then fry the chicken until it begins to brown all over. Season the chicken with pepper but do not add salt, as the salt from the bacon will provide enough for this recipe. Chop up the bacon and garlic and add them to the pan. Fry for a further 3 to 4 minutes. Transfer the contents of the frying pan to the casserole dish and pour in the wine. Add the bay leaf, cover the dish and cook in the oven for 1 hour.

Remove the roots from the shallots and peel but leave them whole. Boil the shallots in unsalted water for 10 minutes then transfer to a frying pan. (NB: the cooking water from the shallots can be bottled and saved to use as stock on another occasion.) Fry the shallots until they are just beginning to brown then add the sliced courgette and fry for a further 3 to 4 minutes until slightly brown on either side. Transfer the shallots and courgettes to the casserole and bake for a further 10 minutes. Serve immediately.

Usage
As a meal for 2 with a suitable accompaniment of potatoes or rice.

Piccalilli

Ingredients (makes 3 to 4 jars)
6 lb (2700 g) of vegetables – roughly: 1 lb 12 oz (790 g) courgette and/or marrow, 14 oz (400 g) cucumber, 3 oz (85 g) calabrese (or cauliflower) florets, 2 oz (55g) climbing beans, 2 oz (55 g) very small onions or shallots.
Salt
1 oz (25 g) mustard powder
1 oz (25 g) ground ginger
1 small piece root ginger
3 oz (85 g) caster sugar
1 pint (500 ml) malt vinegar
1 dessert spoon cornflour
1 dessert spoon turmeric

Equipment
Non-metallic bowl, small plate, preserving pan, wooden spoon, ladle, jam funnel and 3 to 4 jars.

Method
Wash and dice the courgette, marrow and cucumber into suitably small pieces. Layer them in a bowl with salt. Top and tail the beans and cut into short lengths then add them to the bowl. Remove all the stem from the calabrese and cut it into small florets then add it to the bowl with salt. Peel and top and tail the small onions/shallots and leave them whole then add them to the bowl with salt. Place a small plate over the top and weight it down so that it is pressing on the vegetables. Leave for several hours or overnight. Drain off any water, rinse the vegetables under cold running water and dry thoroughly. Add most of the vinegar to the preserving pan, reserving about 3 fl oz (85 ml). Add

the mustard, both gingers and the sugar.   Heat gently, stirring to dissolve the sugar.   When the vinegar begins to steam, start adding the vegetables.   Bring to the boil and simmer for about 5 minutes. Combine the cornflour and turmeric with the reserved vinegar then add it to the pan.   Boil for another 2 to 3 minutes, stirring to thicken. Remove from the heat and ladle into warmed jars and seal immediately.

Storage
Store in a cool, dry place for 2 to 3 months to allow the flavours to develop. Use within a year.

Usage
As you would use conventional piccalilli – with cold meats, salads and in sandwiches.

Mustard Chutney

Ingredients (makes 4 to 5 jars)
1½ lb (700 g) courgette
2½ lb (1100 g) onion
Salt
½ pint (300 ml) white wine vinegar
4½ oz (125 g) caster sugar
1 tsp celery salt
1 tsp turmeric
1 in (2.5 cm) piece of root ginger (peeled and grated)
2 tsp mustard powder
1 tsp mustard seed

Equipment
Non-metallic bowl, small plate, preserving pan, wooden spoon, ladle, jam funnel and 4 to 5 jars.

Method
Wash and dice the courgette into suitably small pieces; layer it in a bowl with salt. Peel and finely chop the onions and layer it in the bowl with salt. Place a small plate over the top and weight it down so that it is pressing on the vegetables. Leave it for several hours or overnight. Drain off any water, rinse the vegetables under cold running water and dry thoroughly. Add the vinegar to the preserving pan with the other ingredients. Heat gently, stirring to dissolve the sugar.   When the vinegar begins to boil add the vegetables. Simmer for about 45

minutes, stirring occasionally until the liquid has almost disappeared. Remove from the heat and ladle into warmed jars and seal immediately.

Storage
Store in a cool, dry place for 2 to 3 months to allow the flavours to develop. Use within a year.

Usage
This is similar in appearance and taste to piccalilli, although milder. It is a useful recipe because it requires less variety of vegetables. It can be used with cold meats, salads and in sandwiches.

Multicoloured Autumn Relish

Ingredients (makes 3 to 5 jars)
1 lb (450 g) green tomatoes
8 oz (225 g) red tomatoes
2 red peppers
2 green peppers
2 sticks celery
2 onions
½ cucumber (peeled)
½ small red cabbage
1 cob's worth of sweetcorn
Salt
8 oz (225 g) light brown sugar
25 fl oz (710 ml) white wine vinegar

Equipment
Non- metallic bowl, small plate, sieve, preserving pan, wooden spoon, ladle, jam funnel and 3 to 5 jars.

Method
Chop all the ingredients into small chunks and layer in the bowl with the salt. Place a small plate over the vegetables and weight down. Leave it for several hours or overnight. Drain and thoroughly rinse and dry the vegetables. Add the vegetables to the preserving pan with the sugar and vinegar. Bring to the boil and simmer for about an hour, stirring occasionally, until the vegetables are tender and the liquid has reduced considerably. Transfer into warmed jars and seal immediately.

Storage
Store in a cool, dry place for 1 month to allow the flavours to develop. Use within a year.

Usage
This striking relish is suitable for use as a condiment with cold meat and cheese and is ideal on hot sandwiches and burgers.

Red Relish

Ingredients (makes 3 to 5 jars)
1½ lb (675 g) red tomatoes
2 red peppers (optional)
2 sticks celery
2 red onions
2 beetroots
½ small red cabbage
8 oz (225 g) red grapes
Salt
8 oz (225 g) light brown sugar
25 fl oz (710 ml) cider vinegar

Equipment
Non- metallic bowl, small plate, sieve, preserving pan, wooden spoon, ladle, jam funnel and 3 to 5 jars.

Method
Chop all the ingredients into small chunks and layer in the bowl with the salt. If you are using seeded grapes, squeeze each grape gently to remove most of the seeds. Place a small plate over the vegetables and weight down. Leave it for several hours or overnight. Drain and thoroughly rinse and dry the vegetables. Add the vegetables to the preserving pan with the sugar and vinegar. Bring to the boil and simmer for about an hour, stirring occasionally, until the vegetables are tender and the liquid has reduced considerably. Transfer into warmed jars and seal immediately.

Storage
Store in a cool, dry place for 1 month to allow the flavours to develop. Use within a year.

Usage

This attractive relish is suitable for use as a condiment with cold meat and cheese and is ideal on hot sandwiches and burgers.

Guinea Fowl with Carrot, Courgette and Port

Ingredients
2 guinea fowl breast fillets
Salt and pepper
Oil (for frying)
3 shallots
1 courgette
1 small carrot
6 large basil leaves
2 large mint leaves
4 fl oz (115 ml) port
2 tbsp water

Equipment
Baking tray and frying pan.

Method
Preheat an oven to 190 °C, 375 °F, gas mark 5. Season the fillets and place them on the baking tray. Cook in the centre of the oven for 30 to 35 minutes. In the meantime, finely chop the shallots, cut the courgettes into rounds and the carrots into thin sticks. ~~10~~ Ten minutes before the breasts are ready, heat the oil in a frying pan and fry the shallots, courgettes and carrots for 4 to 5 minutes. Add the herbs and fry for a further minute. Add the port and the water, stir to blend and heat through for 3 to 4 minutes. Serve the breasts and spoon a portion of the vegetables on top of each.

Usage
As a meal for two accompanied by potatoes or rice.

Carrot and Orange Cake

Ingredients
5 fl oz (150 ml) oil
4½ oz (125 g) dark brown sugar
2 eggs
1½ tsp vanilla extract
2 oranges

8 oz (225g) carrots
3 oz (75g) sultanas
10 oz (275g) plain flour
1 oz (25 g) wheatgerm
1½ tsp mixed spice
2 tsp baking powder
1 tsp baking soda
1 × 200 g tub of soft cheese
5 oz (150g) icing sugar

Equipment
Large mixing bowl, grater, juicer, potato peeler, sieve, cake tin, cooling rack.

Method
Preheat an oven to 170 °C, 325 °F, gas mark 3. Grate the rind off both oranges and extract the juice; reserve 1 teaspoon of rind and the juice from half an orange for the icing. In a large bowl, beat together the oil, sugar, eggs, vanilla extract, orange rind and juice. Peel the carrots then finely grate them. Add the grated carrot and the sultanas to the bowl and mix in. Sift the flour, spice and raising agents into the bowl then stir in the wheatgerm. Pour the mixture into a greased and lined cake tin. Bake for 60 to 70 minutes until a skewer inserted into the cake comes out clean. Allow the cake to cool in the tin for 10 minutes then cool it on a rack. In the meantime, mix together the soft cheese, reserved juice and rind with the icing sugar until smooth. Once the cake has cooled, cut it in half horizontally and spread the icing between the two halves of the cake and on top.

Usage
Serve a slice, at room temperature, as a snack or as dessert.

Storage
It is best stored in an airtight container in the refrigerator and consumed within 3 days.

Pasta and Pizza Herb Mix

Ingredients
3 tbsp basil leaves
2 tbsp oregano leaves
2 tbsp marjoram leaves
1 tbsp thyme leaves

1 small garlic clove
1 small shallot
1 tbsp black pepper corns
3 tsp coarse salt

Equipment
Blender, baking tray and herb jars

Method
Put all the ingredients in a blender and blend until finely chopped. Lay the mixture thinly on a baking tray and place in a cool oven with the door open until the mixture is dry and crumbly. Transfer into suitable herb jars, crumbling between finger and thumb to make finer if desired.

Storage
Store in a cool, dry and dark place and use as required. Replace after a year, as the flavour will be fading.

Usage
This is an ideal herb mix to use in any tomato dish and, as the name suggests, can add flavour to pasta and pizza dishes. It can also enhance cheese on toast (see recipe below).

Pizza Style Cheese on Toast

Ingredients
2 slices of bread
1 small tomato (or tomato and basil ketchup)
Tomato puree
Pasta and pizza herb mix
Cheese
Any other topping – e.g. ham, sweetcorn, cooked mushroom

Method
Grill the bread well on one side and lightly on the other. On the lightly done side, thinly smear some tomato puree, add some slices of tomato (or a teaspoon of ketchup) and sprinkle the herbs over the top. Add any other toppings. Grate cheese over the top and return to the grill until the cheese has melted and is beginning to brown. Serve immediately.

Usage
As a light lunch or snack.

Fish Seasoning

Ingredients
2 tbsp tarragon leaves
1 tbsp lemon balm leaves
1 tbsp lemon thyme leaves
1 tbsp rosemary leaves
1 tbsp black pepper corns
3 tsp coarse salt

Equipment
Blender, baking tray and herb jars

Method
Put all the ingredients in a blender and blend until finely chopped. Lay the mixture thinly on a baking tray and place in a cool oven with the door open until the mixture is dry and crumbly. Transfer into suitable herb jars, crumbling between finger and thumb to make finer if desired.

Storage
Store in a cool, dry and dark place and use as required. Replace after a year, as the flavour will be fading.

Usage
This is an ideal herb mix to use in fish dishes. It can be simply sprinkled over the fish before steaming or grilling it or it can be added to recipes for fish pie or fish cakes. It is also tasty sprinkled into fish paste or smoked salmon sandwiches.

Sage Seasoning

Ingredients
6 tbsp sage
1 small garlic clove
1 small shallot
1 tbsp black pepper corns
3 tsp coarse salt

Equipment
Blender, baking tray and herb jars

Method

Put all the ingredients in a blender and blend until finely chopped. Lay the mixture thinly on a baking tray and place in a cool oven with the door open until the mixture is dry and crumbly. Transfer into suitable herb jars, crumbling between finger and thumb to make finer if desired.

Storage

Store in a cool, dry and dark place and use as required. Replace after a year, as the flavour will be fading.

Usage

This makes a simple sage seasoning that can be used on and in meat dishes such as pork and chicken. Because the mix already contains salt and pepper, there is no need to add extra.

Variations

The same recipe can be used to make other herb seasoning such as rosemary or thyme.

Garlic Chive Butter

Ingredients

4 oz (110 g) butter
2 tbsp finely chopped garlic chive leaves

Equipment

Small bowl and an ice cube tray.

Method

The butter needs to be at room temperature and fairly soft. Add the chives to the butter and stir until well combined. Transfer into an ice cube tray and freeze.

Storage

Once frozen, remove from the tray, bag and return to the freezer until required. Each cube makes a convenient sized portion that can be removed individually.

Usage

Can be used straight from the freezer in hot dishes or thawed first. It is tasty if used to butter a corn on the cob or baked potato; it can be used to fry with or to spread on bread or toast.

Variations
Any herb can be frozen this way but useful variations include chive butter and parsley butter.

Subsequent Years

Things to do

Fruit
If you plan to prune any of your fruit trees or bushes, this is a good time to do it. Pruning is only necessary to adjust the size and shape of your plant, so only do it if you wish to train your plant or if it is getting too big. Some trees, such as plums and cherries should be pruned now before leaf fall because they are more prone to disease if pruned when dormant.

Things to harvest
Apples
Pears
Plums

Preserving Tips
Apples or pears store well if packed in shallow boxes without the fruit touching and stored somewhere cool, dry and frost-free. However, for softer fruit such as plums and for windfall fruit, it is best to peel, cut and cook the fruit until soft before freezing in batches.

In the kitchen

Beetroot and Apple Chutney

Ingredients (makes 5 to 6 jars)
2 lb (900 g) raw beetroot
1 lb (450 g) onions
1½ lb (700 g) apples
1 lb seedless raisins
1½ pints (900 ml) malt vinegar
2 lb (900 g) sugar
2 tsp ground ginger

Equipment
Food processor/cheese grater, preserving pan, wooden spoon, ladle, jam funnel and 5 to 6 jars.

Method
Top, tail and peel the fruit and vegetables. Either grate all the fruit and vegetables or finely chop them in a food processor. Add all the ingredients to the pan and bring to the boil. Simmer for 1 to 1½ hours, stirring occasionally, until thick (see Equipment and Techniques chapter). Transfer into warmed jars and seal immediately.

Storage
Store in a cool, dry place for 1 month to allow the flavours to develop. Use within a year.

Usage
This tasty chutney is suitable for use with cold meat and cheese but goes particularly well with sausages, pork and in ham sandwiches.

October

The first frosts mark the end of the summer season and things quickly move into autumn. This is the month for harvesting the last of the tender crops and beginning the winter clear up. It is also the month to start thinking about next year!

Every year

Things to do

Asparagus
Cut down the asparagus ferns now to prevent damage caused by wind rock over the winter. The ferns can be cut right back to soil level and the foliage can be shredded and composted.

Autumn onions
Autumn onion sets should arrive now and need to be planted straight away.

Broad bean
Broad beans can be sown now to over winter and to give a slightly earlier crop next year. If you have suitable cloches then protection would be a good idea although it is not always necessary.

Carrots
Carrots can be sown now and protected over winter with fleece to provide an early crop next year.

Garlic
Garlic can be planted now. Split the bulbs into it individual cloves and plant each one separately.

Herbs
Deadhead and cut back herbs to tidy up for winter. Chives can be dug up, divided with a spade and replanted as several plants.

Potatoes
Continue to harvest main crop potatoes during this month.

Pumpkins
Don't forget to carve a Halloween lantern from a pumpkin in time for 31st October.

Seed catalogues

If you ordered seeds out of catalogues in the winter/spring, then those companies will automatically send you new catalogues now. Have a look through them and start to decide what you might like to grow next year.

Soil

Cover the ground as it becomes vacant to prevent weeds growing.

Tender crops

It is important to keep an eye on the weather forecast now and harvest all the tender crops before the first frosts arrive. Even if some things are under ripe it is probably worth picking them now and allowing them to continue ripening indoors or to use them under ripe. Placing a banana close to unripe fruit helps to ripen them because the banana emits a chemical (ethylene) that stimulates ripening. It is a bit of a gamble whether to leave unripe tender crops outside in the hope that the frost won't be severe enough to kill them off, or bring them in when still unready.

Once the frosts have arrived and killed off these plants it is worth clearing them away. As the weather gets worse, any plants left will become very soft and mushy and be difficult and unpleasant to clear away.

Things to expect

Autumn crops

All your autumn crops should be growing away strongly by now and some will be ready to harvest, such as the turnips.

Autumn onions

Expect to see some signs of green shoots from your onion sets by the end of the month.

Broccoli and kale

Broccoli and kale plants should look well established now and be growing away.

Carrots

Early sown carrots will become progressively more damaged now. The roots may split and will be nibbled by slugs, mice and carrot root fly. It is possible to leave carrots in the ground all winter and harvest when necessary but you have to tolerate the damage. Alternatively, they can all be harvested now and stored in layers in a box of dry sand (see preserving tips).

Florence fennel
Any fennel that was sown in May will start to bolt now. Late sown fennel will still be fine, although it will go mushy if hit by a severe frost.

Things to harvest
Aubergines (until the frosts)
Beans (until the frosts)
Beetroot
Calabrese
Cape gooseberries
Carrots
Celery
Courgettes (until the frosts)
Cucumbers (until the frosts)
Fennel
Haricots (until the frosts)
Leeks
Melons (until the frosts)
Parsnips
Peppers (until the frosts)
Potatoes
Pumpkins (until the frosts)
Red cabbage
Sweetcorn (until the frosts)
Tomatoes (until the frosts)
Turnips
Winter salads

Harvesting Tips

Beans
By now any beans you were leaving to form haricots should be ready. Look for well-swollen pods, which are firm when squeezed. If you are at all unsure if they are ready, open one up and look at the beans inside. Don't wait until the pod becomes dry and papery – if they have gone this far save the beans inside for seeds instead for sowing next year.

Leeks
Leeks may just about be big enough to harvest in October but you may prefer to leave them in the ground until later in the year when they are

bigger and you generally have less to harvest. When small and when the ground is damp leeks can be harvested by being pulled out of the ground with their roots still attached. If the leeks are larger, or the ground firmer, then the leek can be harvested by cutting it off just below ground level with a sharp knife.

Parsnips
Parsnips may be big enough to harvest now, however some believe that the flavour of parsnips improves after the frosts. You may, therefore, prefer to leave them in the ground until after more severe frost and when other crops are scarcer.

Turnips
These should be harvested when about the size of a ping-pong ball. It is best to use the first harvest to thin the crop. Turnip tops can also be eaten as a welcome winter green. As most of the turnip is above ground, it should be possible to simply pull them up to harvest.

Winter Salads
These should be harvested as and when required, removing only a few leaves from each plant at a time and leaving the plant to recover.

Preserving Tips

Cold storage
Carrots and beetroot can be stored for the winter by packing them in layers in a box of dry sand. Carrots dehydrate quickly if left to the open air and quickly become bendy. However, they will store all winter if packed in sand and kept in a cool, dry, frost-free place. They can be removed from storage as required buy digging in the sand to find them. The carrots and beetroot should be relatively clean and dry when stored and damaged roots should not be stored in this way.

In Storage

In the freezer
Broad beans
Calabrese
Climbing beans (possibly)
Fennel
Herbs and herb butter
Peas
Peppers
Strawberries
Sweetcorn

Tomatoes
Ice cream

In the store cupboard
Pickled beetroot
Borscht
Broad bean soup
Chutney
Dried chilli peppers
Pickled cabbage
Pickled cucumber
Pickled gherkins
Dried herbs
Herb mustards
Jam
Jelly
Pickled onions
Pea and bacon soup
Piccalilli
Tomato sauce
Tomato ketchup

In cold storage
Garlic
Melons
Onions
Potatoes
Pumpkins
Shallots

In the kitchen

Vegetable Stock

October is good time to make a few bottles of good quality vegetable stock for use in winter casseroles etc.

Ingredients (makes 3 pints)
1 onion
1 stick of celery
1 carrot
5 or 6 green beans
1 garlic clove

1 in (2.5 cm) piece of root ginger
2 sprigs each of sage, rosemary and thyme
2 bay leaves
Salt and pepper
3 pints (1700 ml) water

Equipment
Saucepan, sieve and 3 bottles.

Method
Peel and coarsely chop the onion and add it to the pan. Snip up the celery, including its leaves and add it to the pan. Wash and coarsely chop the carrots and green beans and add them to the pan. Peel and chop the garlic and ginger. Add the herbs and the seasoning. Pour 3 pints of boiling water into the pan and bring it back to the boil. Simmer for about 20 to 30 minutes with the lid on the pan. Sieve the cooking water into warmed bottles and seal.

Storage
Once the stock has cooled the safety button should have become depressed again. If it has, then the stock can be stored for several months, if not then use within 3 days or freeze in a suitable container.

Usage
In any recipe requiring stock.

Sausage Hotpot

Ingredients (serves 2)
Oil (for frying)
6 bangers
3 rasher of smoked bacon back
1 leek (or 1 medium onion)
8 small turnips
1 beetroot (preferably golden or pink/white variety to prevent staining)
1 carrot
1 pint (600 ml) stock
Fresh herbs (such as rosemary, sage, thyme and bay)
4-5 medium potatoes
Salt and pepper

Equipment
Frying pan and a casserole dish.

Method
Preheat an oven to 180 °C, 350 °F, gas mark 4. Heat the oil in a frying pan. Cut the sausages into quarters and snip up the bacon. Flash fry the sausages and bacon until the sausages are brown all over then transfer to a casserole dish. Cut the leeks into rounds and layer them over the meat. Top and tail and peel the beetroot, carrot and turnips. Layer the vegetables into the dish. Add the herbs and season with salt and pepper. Peel the potatoes and cut into rounds. Layer the potatoes over the top so that they are slightly overlapping and completely cover the ingredients below. Pour the stock over the top and season the potatoes. Cover with foil or the lid and cook for 1 hour. Remove the foil and continue to cook for a further 40 to 50 minutes until the potatoes are golden brown and crispy. Serve immediately.

Usage
Serves 2 as a complete, filling meal.

Chicken and Vegetable Pie

Below is a suggested recipe for a chicken and vegetable pie. Clearly, the actual vegetables used in this pie will depend on your own preferences and which vegetables you have available. However, I feel it is essential to the flavour of the pie to include leeks.

Ingredients (makes 4-6)
1 small chicken
Fresh sage
1 medium onion
Salt and pepper
1 small carrot
2 turnips
3 or 4 mushrooms
Frozen peas and/or sweetcorn
2 leeks
1 oz (25g) butter
1 oz (25 g) flour
Milk
1 block ready-made puff pastry

Equipment
Roasting tin, 2 to 3 small saucepans, 4-6 pie-cases, rolling pin, and pastry brush.

Method

Preheat an oven to 190 °C, 375 °F, gas mark 5. Peel and coarsely chop the onion and the sage and mix them together with the salt and pepper. Stuff the chicken with this mix then cook the chicken for the required time – approximately 1 to 1½ hours. In the meantime, peel and dice the carrots and turnips and boil them together for 1 to 2 minutes. Dice the mushrooms. Chop the leeks into rounds and boil for 8-10 minutes, retaining the cooking water. In a saucepan, melt the butter and add the flour to it, stirring constantly until it forms a dough ball. Add the leek cooking water, stirring constantly, to make a white sauce. When the chicken is cooked, add the juices from the meat to the white sauce to make gravy and thin it if necessary with milk. The pies require either the meat from two breasts or two legs. It is your decision which meat you put in the pie and what you do with the remaining meat (candelit dinner for two with roast potatoes, veg de jour, dry white wine, and heaps of dessert, anyone?). Cut the meat into small pieces and combine all the vegetables and the gravy. Distribute the filling evenly between the 4 pie cases. Roll out the pastry and cut out a lid for each pie. Place a lid on each pie.

Storage

The pies can be cooked straight away, refrigerated for up to 3 days or frozen until required.

Usage

Cook the thawed pies in a preheated oven at 180 °C, 375 °F, gas mark 5. Glaze the pastry with milk or egg white just before cooking. Cook for 30 to 40 minutes until the pastry has risen and browned. Serve with a suitable accompaniment of potatoes and vegetables.

Home-made Baked Beans

Ingredients

14 oz (400 g) haricot beans
Oil (for frying)
1 medium onion
1 tsp mustard powder
2 tsp soft dark brown sugar
1 tsp black treacle
2 tsp lemon juice
1 tsp Worcestershire sauce
Salt
1 jar of tomato sauce for pasta (see August)

Equipment
Saucepan, casserole dish, frying pan and jars.

Method
Preheat an oven to 150 °C, 300 °F, gas mark 2. Cook the haricot beans in lightly salted water for 20 minutes then drain well and place them in a casserole dish. Peel and finely chop the onions. Heat the oil in a frying pan then fry the onion until soft. Add the tomato sauce and other ingredients to the pan and heat through. Pour the sauce over the beans, put the lid on and bake for 1 hour, stirring occasionally. Add more water if it looks dry or remove the lid for a while if it looks too wet. Remove the dish from the oven, taste and adjust the seasoning if necessary. Transfer to warmed jars of suitable sizes and seal immediately.

Storage
Store in a cool, dry place for a month before opening. Consume within a year.

Usage
As you would normally use baked beans. This is definitely not one of the famous 57 varieties!

Subsequent Years

In the kitchen

Jam Recipes

If you are lucky, by now you have a store cupboard full of a variety of different jams and, despite eating some on your toast every morning, you are not making much of an impression on your stores. Below are a few recipes requiring jam (of any variety) that you might like to try and are in addition to specific jam recipes given in other chapters. They are particularly good to try when you have friends over so that you can show off your talents – homemade desserts with homemade jam from homegrown fruit – very impressive!

Jam Tart Selection

Ingredients
4 oz (110 g) plain flour

4 oz (110 g) wholemeal flour (or a total of 8 oz, 225 g plain flour)
4 oz (110 g) butter or margarine
4 oz (110 g) caster sugar
Water
Jam

Equipment
Sieve, bowl, rolling pin, pastry cutter, foil tart cases, tart tin, and wire rack.

Method
Preheat an oven to 190 °C, 375 °F, gas mark 5. Sift the flours into a bowl, returning any bran to the bowl. Add the fat and rub in with your fingertips until it forms a crumbly texture. Stir in the sugar. Add a few splashes of cold water to bind and knead it into dough. Flour a flat surface and roll the pastry out until about ¼ inch (½ cm thick). Use a pastry cutter to cut out circles of pastry and transfer them into foil tart cases. Place the cases into a tart tin. Place a heaped teaspoon of jam into each case then cook in the oven for 15 to 20 minutes until the pastry is cooked and the jam is molten. Remove from the oven and top up each tart with jam whilst still hot. Cool the tarts in the tin for 5 minutes then transfer onto a wire rack to cool completely.

Storage
Best eaten within a day or two of making but will keep for up to 3 days in an airtight container.

Usage
These can be eaten as a snack or for a dessert. It is particularly good if you can use a selection of jams in the tarts. It is very useful as a tasting opportunity should you wish to sell or give away your excess jams to friends, relatives, colleagues or neighbours.

Jam Sponge Puddings

Ingredients (makes 2)
2 oz (55 g) self-raising flour
½ tsp baking powder
2 oz (55 g) margarine
2 oz (55 g) caster sugar
1 egg
2 drops vanilla essence
Jam

Equipment
Sieve, bowl, and 2 ramekins or small pudding bowls.

Method
Preheat an oven to 170 °C, 325 °F, gas mark 3. Sift the flour and baking powder into a bowl. Add the margarine, sugar, egg and vanilla essence. Mix together until it forms a creamy texture. Put 1 to 2 teaspoons of jam into the bottom of each ramekin. Divide the batter between the 2 ramekins and bake in the oven for about 20 minutes until golden brown and cooked through.

Storage
Can be stored in the refrigerator for 2 to 3 days and reheated as required. If reheating in the microwave be very careful because the jam will get very hot.

Usage
Serve hot either in the ramekin or turned out with custard, cream or evaporated milk as a filling dessert.

Mini Jam-filled Pancakes

Ingredients (makes 10 - 20)
4 oz (110 g) plain flour
Pinch of salt
1 egg
½ pint (300 ml) milk
Jam

Equipment
Sieve, bowl, wooden spoon or whisk, ladle, and frying pan.

Method
Sieve the flour and salt into a bowl and make a well in the centre. Beat the egg into the milk and gradually add the mixture to the flour, stirring as you go. Stir or whisk until a smooth batter is formed. Heat a little oil in a small frying pan. Ladle a little batter into the pan and swirl round until a thin layer of batter covers the base. Cook on one side, turn and cook on the other until golden. Smear with the jam, roll up and serve immediately.

Storage
The batter can be made in advance and stored in the refrigerator for up to 24 hours. It may begin to separate and needs to be stirred well before using.

Usage
As a filling dessert for all the family. This recipe is most appealling if the pancakes are as small as possible (e.g. 3 in, 7.5 cm in diameter). The small size of the pancakes makes them more attractive to children, makes portion control easier and gives an opportunity for a wider range of jams to be sampled. Pancakes this small can be made by using pans or rings designed for cooking fried eggs.

Swiss Roll

Ingredients (makes 1)
3 eggs
4 oz (110 g) caster sugar
3 oz (85 g) plain flour
1 tbsp boiling water
Jam

Equipment
Greaseproof paper, swiss roll tin, electric whisk, sieve, wire rack.

Method
Preheat an oven to 200 °C, 400 °F, gas mark 6. Grease and line a 12 by 8 inch (30 by 20 cm) swiss roll tin. Put the eggs and sugar in a bowl and whisk until it is thick and mousse like and forms soft peaks. Be patient, even with an electric whisk this may take 20 minutes or more. Sift the flour over the top and fold in. Fold in the water. Spoon the mix into a tin and spread out evenly. Bake for 10 to 12 minutes until springy to the touch. Spread a sheet of greaseproof paper onto a flat surface and sprinkle with sugar. Turn out the cake onto this paper and carefully peel off the cooking paper. Smear with jam then carefully roll up the cake whilst still hot. Hold the cake in the rolled up position for a minute or two with the seal underneath. Transfer onto a wire rack to cool completely. When cool, trim of the edges to neaten.

Storage
In an airtight container for up to 3 days.

Usage
As a snack or dessert.

November

By November autumn is definitely here and things are winding down for the winter. This is when you find out whether your preparations during the summer were adequate – are your autumn crops growing, is your freezer stuffed with frozen fruit, vegetables and prepared dishes, is your store cupboard heaving with jarred preserves and do you have things in cold storage? No? All being well you should have a few delights to show for the work you put in during the summer but at least these days if things don't go to plan we can resort to the shops rather than face starvation!

First year

Things to do

Fruit
Now is the best time to plant fruit trees, bushes and canes. Before buying any fruit plants it is important to decide where they will be planted. As with choosing vegetables, it is advisable not to grow fruit if you do not like it or will not have the time or enthusiasm required to deal with the likely glut. In addition, you need to make sure you have suitable sites for them and the space. As fruit plants will grow for many years, it is more important to make the correct decisions now about variety and site and to prepare the ground well than it is for vegetables. If you are intending to grow fruit on an allotment site, check in your tenancy agreement that it is permitted. You may consider some of the following fruit.

Apple
Apples are very versatile fruit and can be eaten from midsummer to mid-spring if more than one type is grown and with correct storage of the fruit. Early and some second early types can be harvested and eaten straight from the tree, whilst mid and late season varieties benefit from storage before being eaten. Apples need a sunny, preferably sheltered position in a well-drained soil. They can be grown as a freestanding tree or trained into a number of different shapes and thus can take up different amounts of space depending on how it is trained. They can even be grown in pots if the correct rootstock (e.g. M27 or M9) is chosen and the plant kept trained. It is best to decide how the tree will be grown before buying it so the correct type of tree can be chosen, including, if your budget will stretch to it, a pre-trained plant. Before planting, suitable support needs to be erected. Water your tree well before planting. Dig a hole slightly larger than the

rootball. Place the tree in the hole. Add slow release fertiliser granules to the soil from the hole then fill in the hole. Firm the tree in well and stake or tie to its support as desired. It is useful if you can mulch around the tree to help preserve moisture and to improve the soil structure but make sure it does not touch the trunk of the tree as this can encourage disease. Alternatively, you can plant the tree through horticultural black plastic that will not only conserve water but also suppress weeds.

Blackberry

Blackberries and their hybrids (e.g. loganberries and tayberries) are grown as canes. They are long whispy stems that bear fruit on side stems. Blackberries can remain productive for up to 15 years so it essential to site them well and to prepare the ground properly. They need to be sheltered from strong winds and, although they like full sun, they will tolerate partial shade. They require good drainage and benefit from the addition of compost to the soil. It is best to dig the soil over first so that weeds are removed. Blackberries are usually maintained as individual plants and trained up single supporting structures, such as an obelisk or arch, and the support should be erected at the time of planting. They will need about 8 feet (2.5 m) of space and need to be planted 3 in (8 cm) deep.

Blueberry

Blueberries are attractive plants with small, white flowers in the spring, blue fruit in the summer and vibrant autumn colour. They need acid soil to grow. Although it is possible to acidify soil, it takes considerable time and effort so it is easier to grow a blueberry in a pot of ericaceous compost if the soil is unsuitable. If growing in a pot, start with a 2 litre pot and pot on again in a couple of years. This also helps to refresh the compost. They prefer sun or partial shade and are relatively tolerant of frost. Look out for self-fertile varieties or plant more than one type.

Cherry

It is very common to find cherry trees growing in gardens and in streets but these are largely ornamental varieties with pink blossom and insignificant, inedible fruit. Therefore, when looking to buy a cherry tree it is important to ensure it is a fruiting variety. There are two types of fruiting cherry – sweet and acid cherries – both of which have white blossom. The sweet cherries are suitable to eat straight from the tree, whilst the acid cherry need to be cooked or made into preserves before being pleasant to eat. Sweet cherry trees are large, vigorous trees that may be unsuitable for small gardens because they are difficult to train. Acid cherries are less vigorous and can be trained, so are more suitable for small gardens. Both types of cherry enjoy a warm position as they flower early and are susceptible to late frosts. The method of planting a cherry tree is the same as for an apple (see above).

Cranberry
Cranberries are low growing, sprawling plants that like slightly acidic boggy conditions. If you don't naturally have these conditions, by preparation of the planting area it is possible to create a suitable environment. To do this, dig out a hole 3 feet (1 m) square to a spade's depth. Line the hole either with horticultural plastic or with ordinary plastic with a few drainage holes pierced in it. Then fill in the hole with ericaceous compost and plant the bush into this. Cranberries grow outwards along the ground so need no support and make excellent ground cover. They are evergreen and the red berries make attractive autumn colour. Assuming the ground is sufficiently acidified, cranberries should not suffer from any pests or problems.

Currants
There are three types of currant commonly grown – black, red and white currants. Although red and white currants can be trained more readily than blackcurrants, it is simplest to grow all types of currant as a bush. All currants like a sheltered, sunny position and will tolerate partial shade. It is important to avoid planting in frost pockets. Red and white currants cannot stand waterlogging, whereas blackcurrants are more tolerate of damp conditions. As these bushes can be viable for up to 10 years, it is important to take care to site them correctly and to prepare the soil well. Dig over the area, removing all weeds and incorporate some well-rotted manure and some slow release, granular fertiliser. Plant the bushes 3 to 5 feet (1 - 1.5 m) apart and just slightly deeper than their rootball. Water well and mulch as for apple trees (see above).

Gooseberry
There are over a hundred gooseberry types currently available. The most obvious difference between gooseberry plants is the colour of the fruit, which can be green, yellow or red. They vary in flavour too from sweet dessert types to more tart ones that need to be cooked to be pleasant to eat. There are also varieties that have a resistance to some of the problems gooseberries can suffer from such as mildew and leaf spot, and some are thornless. It is even possible to have a weeping variety. It is possible to train gooseberries and if you have limited space or poorly drained soil then it a good idea to grow a

gooseberry in a pot trained to a standard or half standard. Gooseberries enjoy a sunny, sheltered position but will tolerate some shade. As they flower early it is best to avoid planting them in a frost pocket. Plant in the same way as currants.

Hazelnut
There are two types of hazelnuts that have a slightly different appearance to the nut but are otherwise very similar. These are cobnuts and filberts. Both grow best in full sun or partial shade. They can easily reach large sizes and need to be pruned heavily each winter to keep them tamed. In most cases, they need to be cross-pollinated to produce a good crop so, unless there are other trees nearby, you will need more than one tree which could be a problem in small gardens. One way round this might be to grow one hazelnut for its fruit and an ornamental corkscrew hazel in a pot. Corkscrew hazels have twisted branches that look very attractive and are restricted by being pot grown to a small size. Plant as you would an apple tree (see above).

Peach
Of all the fruit mentioned here, peaches have to be the most challenging to grow in this country, as they ideally prefer warmer conditions than we can provide. Therefore, it is important to choose the site for your tree carefully so that it is sunny but sheltered and avoids frost. A south-facing wall is the ideal spot. It is also best to choose an early to mid-season variety because the late peach varieties do not do well outdoors. Peach trees vary in size from a medium sized tree to a "patio peach" that is a dwarf tree that can be grown in a pot. Clearly the overall yield on a patio peach will not be as high as on a normal tree but it has the advantages of being able to fit into a small garden and can be moved if necessary. Peach leaf curl is the biggest problem of peaches but it can be prevented if the peach is kept dry during its dormant period over winter and whilst it is flowering. Therefore, it is relatively easy to avoid peach leaf curl on patio peaches because they can be picked up and moved inside over winter (thus also avoiding frost damage) or they can be wrapped in fleece.

Pear
Pears prefer warmer conditions than apples so need to be planted in a sunny, sheltered spot. They will tolerate most soil conditions but do not do well on thin, calcareous soils, such as those over chalk. Pears can be grown simply as trees or trained into a variety of styles that suit the size of the garden they are planted in. Dwarf trees can also be

grown in pots. Plant as for apple trees (see above). Pears suffer from fewer problems than apples.

Plum
Plums are stone fruit that also include damsons and gages. There are no truly dwarf varieties but some are grafted to semi-dwarfing rootstock. Although they can be trained, they are not as amenable to this as apples and pears. Plums blossom early and are, therefore, vulnerable to early frosts so should ideally be planted in a sunny, sheltered position. Planting is done in the same way as for apples and pears.

Raspberry
Raspberries are grown as canes and you will require anything from 4 to 15 canes to produce a usable yield. You may wish to increase the number of canes you grow so that you have more than one variety. This would allow you to grow canes that crop at different times so that you have both summer and autumn harvests, or you might like to consider a yellow raspberry variety for novelty value. The canes are shallow rooted (3 inches, 8 cm deep) and are grown 15 inches (40 cm) apart. It is best to dig the ground over to remove all weeds and to incorporate manure and/or slow release granular fertiliser before planting. They will need to be supported (usually by horizontal wires between posts) but this can be erected by the following autumn so does not have to be done immediately. It is also a good idea to mulch around the canes to suppress weeds.

Every year

Things to do

Asparagus
Now is a good time to mulch your asparagus bed. Pile well rotted manure or compost over the crowns for the winter. This will help to keep the crowns warm and the weeds down as well as adding nutrients to the bed. By the spring, with a bit of luck, the worms would have dragged most of it underground for you.

Carrots and beetroot
Carrots and beetroot sown at the end of the summer will need thinning this month and should be big enough to give you a fresh crop – a relief if pests have damage your old carrots.

Garlic
Garlic can still be planted this month.

Storage
It is important to check your stored crops regularly for any signs of rot. Any rot will quickly spread so the offending item needs to be removed. Start using things you have in storage as your fresh crops dwindle.

Things to expect

Carrots
Carrots sown under fleece last month should have germinated by now. Don't forget to keep them protected against slugs.

Onions and garlic
Onion sets and garlic cloves planted last month should have developed leaves by now.

Soil
With the damp weather your soil will become wet and, if it is clay, sticky. Try to avoid walking on it as it will damage the soil structure as well as mess up your boots! Any roots that you harvest will be very muddy. A neat trick is to take a bucket of warm water and some rubber gloves out when you harvest. Wash the vegetables whilst out there and dispose of the muddy water outside rather than risk clogging up your sink.

Spinach
This should be well established by now and can stand being harvested by removing leaves as and when required.

Things to harvest
Calabrese
Carrots
Beetroot
Celery
Fennel
Kale
Leeks
Parsnips
Potatoes
Red cabbage
Spinach
Turnips
Winter salads

Harvesting Tips

Beetroot leaves
Beetroot leaves can either be harvested at the same time as you harvest the roots, or they can be harvest separately and the roots left to stand in the ground. Either way, to remove the leaves from the root simply twist off. Discard any damaged leaves.

Kale
It is best to pick a few leaves from each kale plant regularly all winter. The plant should cope with losing a few leaves and continuous picking helps to prevent the kale from bolting early in the spring. Because of the curly nature of the leaves, kale tends to collect rainwater and you are very likely to get wet, and probably very cold, fingers when harvesting it.

Spinach
Pick a few leaves from each plant as required.

Cooking Tips

Beetroot leaves
Now that vegetables are scarcer, you may wish to try eating the leaves of beetroot. To do so, treat it as you would spinach.

Kale
Place the whole leaves in a pan of lightly salted water and boil for about 10 minutes until tender. To liven it up a bit you might like to add a few pieces of root ginger to the water as it cooks.

Spinach
Spinach has a very high water content and collapses when cooked so don't underestimate the amount you will need. Place the whole leaves in a steamer and steam for about 10 minutes until tender. Alternatively, heat some oil in the bottom of a saucepan, add the spinach and some salt. Place the lid on the pan and cook for about 30 seconds. Stir it and replace the lid for another 30 seconds. Drain the spinach and press it to drain off any excess water. Season with black pepper and grated nutmeg.

In Storage

In the freezer
Broad beans
Calabrese

Climbing beans (possibly)
Fennel
Herbs and herb butter
Peas
Peppers
Soft fruit
Sweetcorn
Tomatoes
Ice cream

In the store cupboard
Pickled beetroot
Baked beans
Borscht
Broad bean soup
Chutney
Dried chilli peppers
Pickled cabbage
Pickled cucumber
Pickled gherkins
Dried herbs
Herb mustards
Jam
Jelly
Pickled onions
Pea and bacon soup
Piccalilli
Tomato sauce
Tomato ketchup
Vegetable stock

In cold storage
Apples
Beetroot
Carrots
Garlic
Melons
Onions
Pears
Potatoes
Pumpkins
Shallots

In the kitchen

Red Cabbage and Ginger

Ingredients
Red cabbage
Root ginger
Salt

Equipment
Saucepan

Method
Slice a suitable quantity of red cabbage into strips and place in a saucepan of lightly salted water. Peel and coarsely chop some root ginger and add it to the saucepan. Boil together for 10 minutes until the cabbage is tender. Drain and serve immediately.

Usage
As a side dish.

Home-made Pizza

Homemade pizza is an excellent way to use up some of your homemade tomato sauce for pasta or frozen tomatoes and some of your other frozen vegetables. Below is a suggestion of suitable toppings but obviously the choice is down to you.

Ingredients (makes 2 to 4)
Pre-made pizza bases (any size)
1 jar of tomato sauce for pasta (or ingredients for topping, see below)
Cheese (preferably mozzarella/cheddar mix)
2 rashers of bacon or ham
2 mushrooms
Frozen sweetcorn
Frozen peppers
1 shallot or small onion

If making your own pizza topping you will require:
Oil (for frying)
1 medium onion
1 garlic clove
1 lb (450 g) frozen tomatoes (thawed)

4 tsp tomato puree
Dried herbs or some pasta and pizza herb mix (see September)
A few drops of lemon juice

Equipment
Cheese grater, scissors, and baking tray. Plus a frying pan if making your own topping

Method
Preheat an oven to 220 °C, 425 °F, gas mark 7. To make your own pizza topping, heat the oil in a frying pan, chop the onions finely and fry for 3 to 4 minutes until soft. Add the crushed garlic and stir for another minute then remove from the heat. Pinch the skins of the thawed tomatoes and squeeze out the pulp into the frying pan. Sprinkle some dried herbs into the pan and add the tomato puree and the seasoning. Bring to the boil then simmer for 20 to 25 minutes until thick and pulpy; stir occasionally but more frequently towards the end. Add the lemon juice then allow the topping to cool. Spread the sauce over the pizza bases. Grate the cheese and sprinkle evenly over the bases. Cook the bacon and snip it into piece with scissors. Add the toppings to the pizzas. Cook for 10 to 20 minutes (depending on size) on a greased baking tray.

Storage
It is best to use all the sauce in one go because it does not keep for long once opened. It is therefore best to make up surplus pizzas and freeze. If doing this, ensure that the frozen vegetables don't thaw out whilst making up the pizzas. Once made, freeze them uncovered until fully frozen then transfer into bags. If you attempt to freeze them in bags straight away you will dislodge the toppings and get the sauce on the bag. The pizzas can be cooked from frozen or thawed first.

Usage
As a meal or snack depending on their size.

Subsequent Years

Fruit
Now that the leaves have fallen and you can see what you are doing you may want to prune your fruit bushes and trees. Most fruit bushes can be propagated from cuttings so if you do prune them perhaps consider propagation too. It is, however, best to avoid pruning stone fruit trees (plums, cherries and peaches, for example) at this time of year as they become prone to infection once their sap lowers.

Mulch around the base of currants and berries using well-rotted manure and compost.

Gather fallen leaves and add them to your compost bin.

Spray peach trees with a copper-based fungicide to help prevent leaf curl next year, then wrap it up in fleece to keep it protected from the cold or bring it indoors.

December

In the cold, short days of December there is very little that you can do on your plot but it is an excellent time for planning next year and thumbing through seed catalogues. It is also a time for celebration and some of your summer fare can be given away as presents. And with any luck, you will have enough fresh produce still growing and things in storage to put together an impressive Christmas dinner. Don't forget all those pickles and chutneys when it comes to cold meat dinners and sandwiches!

Every year

Things to do

Christmas presents
Every December I check through my store cupboard of jams, chutneys and pickles and decide who would appreciate receiving a few jars for Christmas. Although I'm sure friends and relatives would appreciate the jars as they are, I believe a little bit of time spent on presentation makes the present even more special. Because I use a variety of old jars of different shapes and sizes they can looks like a bit of a hotchpotch when put together as a present. However, this is easily improved by producing some designer labels. Firstly, it is important to make sure that the jars are clean and that you remove any hand written labels you just stuck on so you wouldn't forget what it was. Next, buy or make some attractive labels. I use a computer to produce my labels so that they are produced quickly and are consistent in design and size. The labels are made from ordinary paper and stuck on with normal stick glue. Please note, however, that inkjet printer ink does run if it gets wet. I make one label for the side of the jar and a circular label for the lid to cover up any product name on there. When giving away more than one jar to one person, I like to put the jars in a cardboard box covered in wrapping paper or in a basket. Not only does this improve the appearance of the present but also it makes it easier to wrap and handle than loose jars. I also have an arrangement with friends and relatives that as they use up their gifts they will return the jars and the basket to me for refilling for the following Christmas. This makes the whole process very cheap and environmentally friendly!

Clear up
With very little else needing doing on the plot during this month, it is a good time to finish the clear up so that it is ready for the spring.

Tender crops will have been killed by the first frosts but will become soft and squishy when hit by severe frosts or snow, so it is best to clear these before the job becomes very unpleasant. If you have heavy clay soil it is advisable to avoid walking on it at this time of year. Not only will it stick to your boots but also you will damage the soil structure. It can be desirable to cover the soil with black plastic or carpet over winter to stop weeds growing on it. Light soils particularly benefit from this because winter rains can leach nutrients out of the soil. However, clay soil does benefit from being exposed to frosts because this helps to break the soil down into fine pieces. So with heavy soils it's best to wait until late winter or even early spring, when the weeds are just beginning to show, then cover the soil with plastic or carpet. Ideally, by the end of the winter you want your plot to be ready and waiting for the planting, with no debris to clear and soil ready for sowing.

The clear up should also continue inside too. Wash pots and disinfect if you wish. Clean reusable labels. Wash out the inside of your cold frame too. Pots and cold frames can carry fungal spores that may lead to "damping off" of seedlings next year. This is when the thin stem of a seedling collapses for no apparent reason (although in reality it is due to fungal infection) and the seedling dies. Although it is sometimes unavoidable, good hygiene helps to prevent it.

Crop rotation
When you start to plan next year's planting season don't forget to take crop rotation into account. Each plant takes specific nutrients out of the soil and is vulnerable to specific soil-born pests and diseases. By avoiding planting the same thing in the same soil each year, the soil has chance to recover its nutrients and the pests and diseases do not build up. There are specific rules about what type of crop should follow from another. Crops can be grouped into four broad groups: legumes (beans and peas), brassicas (broccoli, calabrese, kale, cabbage), roots (carrots, beetroot, parsnips, potatoes) and others (e.g. tomatoes, peppers, leeks, onions, sweetcorn etc.). In theory, brassicas should follow legumes or others, and roots should follow brassicas. However, this is not always practical. Different crops take up different amounts of space and the land becomes available at different times of the year. For example, it might be practical to follow first early potatoes with winter brassicas simply because the ground is ready at that time. I would recommend ignoring the general rules and simply avoid planting the same crop in the same place in successive years. However, there are some other considerations you might like to take into account, as follows.

Legumes (beans and peas) add nitrogen to the soil so provide a fertile soil for leaf growth for the next crop.

Potatoes, cucurbits and beans all do well in freshly manured ground. However, carrots fork if placed in freshly manured ground. So, if you have added manure to your plot think about what would benefit most and wait until the next season to plant carrots there.

Brassicas prefer the soil to be limed before planting but potatoes form scab if planted in a limed soil. Similarly, digging out potatoes loosens the soil and brassicas need to be planted in a firm soil. Root crops, such as parsnip and carrot like a deeply dug soil.

Tomatoes and potatoes belong to the same family and both suffer from blight so should not follow on from each other.

Turnips, mustard and rocket are also brassicas.

Perennial crops such as asparagus, rhubarb, and fruit should not be moved so are not included in the crop rotation.

Digging
If you have avoided walking on the soil all year you should find that you have to do very little digging. In fact, digging as you remove crops such as potatoes should be sufficient. In some cases, where the crop is not dug out, it may be necessary to fork the soil over and remove any plant debris as you go. Avoid digging if the soil is very wet and heavy. Not only does it make it hard work but it does not help the soil structure. Once the area is cleared, either leave the soil exposed to the frosts or cover it up to prevent weeds growing. It is surprising that even in the cold months perennial weeds such as dock and couch grass will grow, albeit slower than they did in July!

Storage
Keep checking your stored produce for signs of rot and discard any offending items. Keep using stored produce because it will deteriorate. Some things, such as pumpkins and melons, need to be used up by Christmas whilst others can continue to be stored until February/March.

In Storage

In the freezer
Broad beans

Calabrese
Climbing beans (possibly)
Fennel
Herbs and herb butter
Peas
Peppers
Strawberries
Sweetcorn
Tomatoes
Ice cream

In the store cupboard
Pickled beetroot
Borscht
Broad bean soup
Chutney
Dried chilli peppers
Pickled cabbage
Pickled cucumber
Pickled gherkins
Dried herbs
Herb mustards
Jam
Jelly
Fruit cheese
Pickled onions
Pea and bacon soup
Piccalilli
Tomato sauce
Tomato ketchup

In cold storage
Beetroot
Carrots
Garlic
Melons
Onions
Potatoes
Pumpkins
Shallots

In the Kitchen

Although fresh fruit and vegetables are scarce at this time of the year, it is still possible to use some of your own produce in party food. Below are a few recipe ideas that you might like to use to show off your produce, should you host a Christmas party requiring buffet food or even a sit down meal requiring starters and desserts. The recipes use produce that is either available fresh during December or is in storage.

Cheese and Onion Tarts

Ingredients (makes 10)
2 oz (55 g) self-raising flour
2 oz (55 g) wholemeal flour
½ tsp mustard powder
Pinch of salt
2 oz (55 g) margarine
1½ oz (43 g) grated cheese
2 medium onions
1 oz (28 g) butter
1 egg
2 fl oz (55 ml) skimmed milk
Black pepper
Grated cheese

Equipment
Sieve, bowl, cheese grater, rolling pin, 4 inch (10 cm) pastry cutter, 10 metal tart cases, greaseproof paper, jam tart baking tray, frying pan, spatula.

Method
Preheat an oven to 190 °C, 375 °F, gas mark 5. Sift the flours, mustard and salt into a bowl. Add the margarine and rub in with your fingertips until it has the consistency of breadcrumbs. Add the grated cheese and enough water to bind it together to make a soft, clean dough. Roll the pastry out on a floured surface until ¼ inch (½ cm) thick. Cut out 10 circles of pastry and place them in individual cases. Put a piece of greaseproof paper in each case and weight it down with bread crusts, rice or similar. Bake the cases for 10 to 15 minutes until the pastry is just cooked. In the meantime, peel and finely chop the onions. Melt the butter in the frying pan and fry the onions for about 20 minutes, stirring occasionally, until browned. Remove the paper from

each pie case and fill each case three-quarters full with onion. Beat the egg and stir in the milk and add some freshly ground black pepper. Pour the egg mix over the onion to fill each case. To finish, top each tart with grated cheese. Bake for 20 to 30 minutes until just beginning to brown.

Storage
Store in the refrigerator for up to 3 days. Alternatively freeze the same day.

Usage
Serve hot or cold at a party or as a starter.

Potato Wedges

Ingredients
Potatoes
Salt
Freshly ground black pepper
Dried herbs
(Crushed garlic)
Olive oil

Equipment
Kitchen towel, bowl, baking tray.

Method
Preheat an oven to 200 °C, 400 °F, gas mark 6. Scrub the potatoes and only peel if the skins are particularly damaged. Cut the potato into chunky wedges, rinse and pat dry with kitchen towel. Place the potatoes in a large bowl. Sprinkle over the seasoning. This should include salt and pepper and some herbs. You may like to use a dried herb mix (see May) and you may wish to add some crushed garlic. Pour some oil over the wedges then toss until the potatoes are thoroughly coated in oil and seasoning; tip out onto a baking tray and arrange in a single layer. Place in the top of the oven and cook for 40 to 45 minutes, turning once. Best served hot.

Storage
These are best eaten immediately but any leftovers can be stored overnight in the fridge and reheated the next day.

Usage
As hot buffet food or as a side dish.

Tasty Chicken Drumsticks

Ingredients
10 to 12 chicken drumsticks
Salt and pepper
Fresh or dried herbs
1 tbsp soy sauce
3 tsp Worcestershire sauce
2 crushed garlic cloves
2 medium shallot, finely chopped
2 cm piece of root ginger, finely chopped
1 tsp celery salt
1 tsp five spice powder
1 tbsp olive oil

Equipment
Bowl, roasting tin and rack

Method
Preheat oven to 190 °C, 375 °F, gas mark 5. Mix together all the ingredients except the chicken in a small bowl. For each drumstick, carefully force up the skin so that a pocket is formed between the skin and the meat. Spoon a small amount of the seasoning mixture into the pocket and smear round under the skin. Once you have done this to all the drumsticks, take each stick and wipe it around the bowl to pick up any remaining seasoning on the outside of the skin. Arrange the drumsticks on a rack above a roasting tin and roast for 30-40 minutes until cooked through and the juices run clear. Serve immediately or allow to cool fully on the rack before transferring into bags and placing them in the refrigerator until required.

Storage
Although these can be stored in the refrigerator for up to 3 days, it is best to eat them either the same day or the following day.

Usage
Serve one or two warm as a starter or as part of a main course. Alternatively, serve cold as part of a buffet.

Smoked Salmon and Calabrese Quiche

At this time of year you may still have a little bit of calabrese remaining. If so then this recipe is a good use of the tiny side shoots that the plant will be producing. It is also a good use of leftover salmon and/or cream from Christmas. If you don't have any leftover salmon then salmon trimmings make a cheap alternative.

Ingredients
For base:
2 oz (55 g) plain flour
2 oz (55 g) wholemeal flour (alternatively use a total of 4 oz plain flour)
1 tsp mustard powder
Pinch of salt
2 oz (55 g) margarine or butter

For filling:
3 oz (225 g) calabrese
2 oz (55 g) smoked salmon
2 eggs
3 fl oz (85 ml) cream
Freshly ground black pepper

Equipment
Two bowls (large and small), sieve, rolling pin, 5-inch flan dish, knife, saucepan, scissors, fork.

Method
Preheat an oven to 200 °C, 400 °F, gas mark 6. Sift the flours, mustard and salt into a bowl, include any bran that remains in the sieve. Add the diced fat and rub it in until the mixture resembles fine breadcrumbs. Add enough cold water to bind the mixture together and form a firm dough ball. Roll the pastry out onto a lightly floured surface and use to line a 5-inch (12 cm) greased flan dish. Blind bake the pastry for 10-15 minutes. In the meantime, boil the calabrese florets in lightly salted water until just tender. Reduce the oven temperature to 190 °C, 375 °F, gas mark 5. Drain the calabrese well and arrange it in the bottom of the flan case. Snip the smoked salmon into small pieces with scissors and arrange it over the calabrese. In another bowl beat together the eggs and the cream and add the pepper and herbs if using. Pour the mixture over the calabrese and salmon so that it is covered. Bake the quiche for about 30 minutes until set; test it with a fork, which should come away clean if it is cooked.

Storage
This is best eaten the same day that it is cooked but it can be frozen or stored in the refrigerator for up to 3 days.

Usage
Cut into portions and serve as part of a main course or as part of a buffet.

Strawberry Cheesecake

This is a good way to use up frozen fruit and gives the taste of strawberries and cream in the middle of winter. It can also be made with other sweet fruits, such as raspberries and blackberries.

Ingredients
Base:
2 to 3 oz (55 to 85 g) crushed digestive biscuits
1 oz (28 g) melted butter

Filling:
7 oz (200 g) soft cheese
3 oz (85 g) caster sugar
1-2 tsp lemon juice
1 egg
4 fl oz (115 g) whipping cream
6 oz (170 g) frozen strawberries (thawed)

Equipment
Rolling pin, flan dish, bowl, wooden spoon, fork, wire rack

Method
To make the base: Crush the biscuits with the end of a rolling pin until finely crumbed. Melt the butter and mix it with the biscuit crumbs. Press the mix firmly into the bottom of a flan dish and chill for about 1 hour.

To make the filling: Preheat oven to 180 °C, 350 °F, gas mark 4. Cream together the cheese and the sugar until light and fluffy. Add the egg, lemon juice and cream and beat with a fork until smooth. Stir in the strawberries then pour the mixture over the base. Bake for 20 to 30 minutes until set. Cool on a rack then cover and refrigerate. Serve chilled.

Storage
Store in the refrigerator for up to 3 days. Alternatively, cut the cake into portions and make sure they can be removed individually from the dish, then freeze. Once frozen, the portions can be removed from the flan dish and stored in a more convenient container. Individual portions can be removed from the freezer about an hour before required and thawed before eating.

Usage
Serve chilled as a dessert.

Melon and Cherry Sticks

Ingredients
¼ melon
10-15 glace cherries

Equipment
Knife, cocktail sticks

Method
Cut the melon into cubes about ½ inch (1 to 1½ cm) square. Thread a cherry onto a cocktail stick then push it into the cube of melon.

Storage
These can be stored in the refrigerator for a few hours but do quickly dry up so are best prepared just before you wish to use them.

Usage
Serve 5 or 6 as a light starter or dessert as part of a formal meal. Alternatively, arrange them on a plate and serve as buffet food.

Christmas Menu Ideas

It's the end of the year. You have worked hard and it is time to celebrate and show off! Here are a few menu ideas (with recipes where required) to make the most out of your fresh produce and your stored preserves.

Christmas Eve

Starter: Homemade soup (from your stores, e.g. borscht, asparagus, pea and ham, broad bean, watercress or celery)

Main Course: Roast beef with herb mustard (see May)
Leeks
Boiled waxy potatoes
Roast parsnip
Leek stock gravy (see February)

To roast parsnips, simply peel them, cut them into large chunks and place them in the roasting tin whilst cooking the meat. They will require about an hour.

Dessert: Strawberry cheesecake (see above)

Christmas Day

Starter: Melon

Main Course: Bird (turkey, duck, goose etc.) stuffed with Christmas stuffing (see below)
Baked carrots
Broccoli and/or kale
Mashed parsnips (see below)
Roast potatoes (see below)
Vegetable stock and meat juice gravy (see below)
Cranberry sauce (see below), or redcurrant, raspberry and sherry jelly (see July)

To bake carrots, peel and cut into strips about 4-inch (10 cm) long and ½-inch (1.5 cm) thick. Wrap in cooking foil with a little oil and salt, black pepper, and fennel or tarragon. Bake for about an hour and a half.

Dessert: For a lighter dessert than the traditional Christmas pudding, try posh preserved strawberry dessert (see June)

Boxing Day

Starter: Winter salad (see below)

Main Course: Roast pork glazed with apple and sage cheese (see August)

> Braised red cabbage (see below)
> Turnips
> Roast potatoes
> Roast shallots

To roast shallots, peel them but leave them whole. Place them in a roasting tin whilst the meat is cooking. They require anything from 1 to 2 hours to cook, depending on how brown you like them.

Dessert: Summer fruit Pavlova – made by spooning some summer fruits in cassis (see July) into individual meringue nest and topping with cream.

The Day After

Main course: Cold meat, or salmon and calabrese quiche (see above)
> Boiled potatoes
> Beetroot
> Frozen peas and/or sweetcorn
> A selection of pickles and chutney

Dessert: Mini pancakes with jam (see October) or fruit crumble (see July or August)

Christmas Stuffing

When I stuff a bird I use two types of stuffing – one to stuff the cavity of the bird that adds flavour to the meat and gravy but is not eaten, and one to stuff the crop that is eaten.

Ingredients
For the cavity:
1 onion
3-4 sprigs of sage
2 bay leaves
1 sprig rosemary
2 oz dried apricots
2 oz mushrooms
1 garlic clove

1 piece of root ginger
Salt and pepper

For the crop:
2 good quality banger size sausages
1 shallot
1 sprig sage

Method
For the cavity: peel and coarsely chop the onion. Chop the apricots, mushrooms, garlic and ginger. Mix all the ingredients together then pack it into the cavity of the bird.

For the crop: Slit the sausage skins and peel off. Mash the sausage meat to break it up. Peel and finely chop a shallot. Add the shallot and sage to the meat and combine well. Stuff into the crop of the bird.

Usage
To stuff any bird from a chicken to a goose – adjusting the quantities if necessary. Once the meat is carved, the carcass and the cavity stuffing can be boiled up to produce a very tasty stock with which to make gravy. The crop stuffing should be sliced, along with the breast meat and served.

Mashed Parsnips

Ingredients
Parsnips
Olive oil
Butter
Salt and pepper

Equipment
Saucepan, bowl and potato masher

Method
Peel and chop the parsnips. Place them in a pan of lightly salted water and boil for 10 to 15 minutes until they are soft. Drain well and transfer to a bowl. Add a knob of butter and a spoonful of olive oil, season, then mash until smooth and serve immediately.

Usage
As a side dish.

Roast Potatoes

Ingredients
Potatoes (preferably a floury type)
Oil, lard or duck/goose fat

Equipment
Saucepan, sieve, roasting dish

Method
Preheat an oven to 190 °C, 375 °F, gas mark 5. Fill a kettle with water and boil. Peel a suitable number of potatoes and cut into quarters. Pour the water into a large pan, salt lightly and bring back to the boil. Add the potatoes and par boil until just beginning to soften. This should take about 10 minutes but will vary depending on the variety of the potato used and the size of the pieces. In the meantime, put enough oil/fat into a roasting tin so that it forms a thin layer across the bottom of the tin when hot. Place the tin in the oven to heat. Drain the potatoes well then return to the pan, place the lid on and give the pan a gentle shake to rough up the surface of the potatoes. Remove the tin from the oven and tip the potatoes in. Turn each potato in the tin so that it is coated in oil. If you are cooking meat with the potatoes, move the potatoes towards the edges of the pan so that the meat does not shelter them from the heat. Cook the potatoes for about 45 minutes. Take the meat out to allow it to rest. In the meantime, turn the oven up to 200 °C, 400 °F, gas mark 6 and move the tin to the top shelf. Turn each potato over then return them to the oven until the meat has been carved (or for 10 minutes if not cooking with meat). Serve immediately.

Usage
As a delicious side dish to a roast dinner.

Vegetable Stock and Meat Juice Gravy

Ingredients
1 jar (or ½ pint, 300ml) vegetable stock
3 heaped tsp flour (cornflour or plain)
1 tsp mustard powder
Juices from roast meat

Equipment
Saucepan, gravy separator.

Method

Make the vegetable stock if necessary (see October) or use a jar from storage. Pour the stock into a pan and heat it until simmering. In a cup or jug, mix together the flour and mustard powder and add enough cold water that it forms a thick liquid. Collect juices from the roasting meat. It is a good idea to collect the first juices about half way through the cooking time of the meat by scraping a spoon across the bottom of the roasting tin. By the end of the cooking time juices can be collected again. However by this point some juices might be burnt. Although a small amount of dark brown juice is useful to add colour to the gravy, avoid using too much as it might give the gravy a bitter taste. After the meat has rested and carved, more juices can be poured off. Try to avoid collecting too much fat when collecting juices. A gravy separator can be handy to help remove the fat. Add the juices to the vegetable stock and bring it to the boil. Pour in the flour mix, stirring continually and bring back to the boil. Boil until a thick gravy has formed. Don't be surprised if it does not form a deep brown coloured gravy, as you might expect if using a beef stock cube or gravy powder. Despite its colour, this makes very taste gravy.

Usage

To pour over a roast dinner.

Cranberry Sauce

Ingredients

1 lb (450 g) fresh or frozen cranberries
6 oz (170 g) granulated or caster sugar
16 fl oz (500 ml) boiling water

Equipment

Saucepan, ladle, jam funnel, jars

Method

Heat a cool oven and place the jars in it to warm. Put all ingredients into a saucepan and cook for about 10 minutes. Ladle the warm sauce into hot jars and seal immediately

Storage

It is a good idea to store this sauce in small jars because it does not store well once opened. Once opened it needs to be used within a week. It can also be frozen but would need to be transferred into a suitable container to do this.

As an accompaniment to the Christmas bird, particularly turkey.

Winter Salad

Ingredients
Oriental salad leaves
Rocket
Spring onions
Carrot
Garlic chives
Salad dressing
Beetroot (cooked)
Parmesan

Equipment
Bowl, potato peeler.

Method
Wash and dry the oriental leaves and rocket. Top and tail the spring onions and cut in half lengthways. Scrub, peel and cut the carrots into matchsticks. Snip the garlic chives. Put all these ingredients in a bowl, add your favourite salad dressing and toss the salad. Peel and slice the beetroot and add to the bowl. Use a potato peeler to make some Parmesan shavings then sprinkle over the salad.

Usage
As a starter or side dish.

Braised Spiced Red Cabbage

Ingredients
1 lb (450 g) red cabbage
1 large onion (red or brown)
1 clove garlic
Pinch freshly grated nutmeg
Pinch cinnamon
Pinch ground cloves
1 tbsp brown sugar
1 tbsp red wine vinegar
1 tbsp oil
Salt and pepper

Equipment
Casserole dish with lid.

Method
Preheat oven to 150 °C, 300 °F, gas mark 2. Discard the outer leaves of the cabbage then coarsely chop the cabbage. Layer the cabbage in the casserole dish; add a layer of chopped onions, sprinkle with the garlic, sugar and spices. Continue to layer like this until all the cabbage is used. Pour the vinegar over the top, followed by the oil and finally the seasoning. Put the lid on the dish and cook it for 1½ to 2 hours, stirring two or three times.

Storage
This dish can be kept warm without spoiling. It is also possible to reheat it so it is best made in advance and kept in the fridge for up to a day. It can also be frozen.

Usage
As a side dish.

Equipment and Techniques

Chutney making
See Jam making section for advice about preserving pans, jar warming and transferring to jars.

Ventilation
Chutney making is literally something that should be done behind closed doors and is not the sort of thing you should try in a studio apartment! When chutney is reducing, pungent vinegary fumes are released which can be quite pervasive. Making chutney is best done on a day when you can have the windows open. It is also better for your health if you can leave the room whilst the chutney is reducing, checking and stirring it occasionally, as it is not advisable to breathe in acid fumes.

Vinegar
You may have noticed that there are a variety of different vinegars on the market. The most common is malt vinegar, which has a dark brown colour. Distilled malt vinegar is colourless but also has a harsher flavour. Pickling vinegar tends to be malt vinegar with added spices and can be extremely tangy. Other vinegars include red and white wine and cider vinegar. The choice of vinegar for a recipe is down to the subtly different flavours they offer and the colour that is produced. For example, cider vinegar is best in fruity recipes as its flavour enhances that of the ingredients and white wine or distilled vinegar is best in recipes with pale ingredients where dark brown vinegar would mask the colours.

Sugar
It is common to use brown sugar in chutney because it adds to the flavour and colour of the end product. Generally, the darker the sugar the stronger the flavour and the colour produced. White sugar is only preferable in recipes where the delicate colour of the vegetables is preserved.

Thickness test
When the chutney is still hot it will be very slightly runnier than when it cools. If you want thick chutney then test it by running a spoon through the middle of it and seeing how long it takes for the groove to infill with vinegar. Chutney is ready when there is a delay or the groove remains.

Jars
Because chutney tends to have a strong flavour, it is one of the few things you can bottle in jars that retain the odour of their previous occupant – things like cooking sauces. I am always most confident when I bottle chutney in jars with "safety buttons" as I know they are properly sealed if the safety button becomes depressed again on sealing. However, most jars will be fine. One word of caution is to avoid jars with exposed metal on the inside because the high vinegar content of the chutney will corrode the metal.

Storage
The flavour of chutney improves with age. I would recommend that most chutney should be stored for about 3 months in order for the flavours to mature and mellow before eating. Immature chutney can have a very harsh flavour. Once opened they can be stored at room temperature or in the refrigerator but the lids must always be well sealed to prevent the vinegar evaporating and the chutney drying out. I would also recommend using chutneys up within a year as the flavours can become a bit tainted by then and the ingredients can become mushy.

Freezing

Blanching
It is debatable whether it is necessary to blanch vegetables before freezing. It is a traditional method and its purpose is no longer entirely clear. However, some people believe that it helps to kill any bacteria on the vegetables, thus preserving them for longer, whilst others insist that the vegetables retain a superior colour and texture if blanched. Some people, on the other hand, believe it is a waste of valuable time and notice little difference between blanched and non-blanched produce. Certainly, I would only recommend blanching for vegetables you intend to eat in the same way as fresh – i.e. not those you only intend to use in casseroles or jams etc.

Blanch vegetables as follows. Prepare a large pan of unsalted water on a rolling boil. Also prepare a bowl or sink full of iced water. Prepare the vegetables as necessary. You will need some quick way of moving the vegetables from place to place, such as a metal sieve or a steamer insert. In batches, put the vegetables into the sieve and plunge the sieve into the boiling water. Leave it there for a minute or two until you see a distinct change in colour, such as the vegetables becoming a brighter green. It may be necessary to rotate the vegetables in the water so that all of it changes colour. Then remove the sieve from the pan and empty its contents into the iced water to cool. Once cool, removed from the iced water and allow to drain and dry if possible.

Freezing
Ideally, the vegetables should be frozen in open trays in the freezer so that they freeze separately before being stored in bags. This allows appropriate sized portions to be removed, without having to break up huge frozen lumps. Alternatively, the vegetables can be frozen in portion sizes in bags.

Suitable fruit, vegetables and herbs

Apple (cooked as a pie filling)
Asparagus (for use in soups)
Broad beans
Broccoli
Calabrese
Cape gooseberries (for use in jams)
Carrots
Chives
Currants (for use in jams/crumbles)
Florence fennel
Gooseberries (for use in jams and other recipes)
Leeks (for use in stocks and casseroles)
Mint
Parsnips
Peas
Peppers (for use on pizzas and in other dishes)
Potatoes (mashed)
Raspberries (for use in jams and other recipes)
Rosemary
Sage
Savory
Strawberries (for use in jams and other recipes)
Sweetcorn (loose or on the cob)
Thyme
Tomatoes (for use in sauces etc.)

Jam making

Preserving pan
It is essential that you get yourself a preserving pan to make jam in. You may think that any old large saucepan will do but even large

saucepans are not big enough to accommodate jam when it is boiling vigorously. My first experience of making jam was in what I thought was a large pan. I set the jam to boil then went to water some plants on my windowsill and when I looked back sticky red liquid was gushing onto my cooker hob. It looked like someone had been murdered! Preserving pans have a huge capacity and are very useful for jam making, pickles, sauces and soups and just boiling up large quantities of vegetables in one go. Check to see whether a relative such as your mother or grandmother has one that they no longer use. Failing that, you can buy them from a variety of places such as ironmongers, large department stores (e.g. John Lewis), or mail order catalogues (e.g. Lakeland Limited). Remember: the sooner you wash up the preserving pan, the easier it is!

Pectin
Pectin is a substance found naturally in fruit and it is the stuff that makes the jam set. Some fruits are low in pectin (e.g. strawberries), some have medium pectin content (e.g. plums) and others are high in pectin (e.g. currants and gooseberries). Making jam with high pectin fruit is easy and it becomes progressively more difficult the lower the pectin. High pectin fruit will need to be boiled with water whilst low pectin fruit will require no water to be added. High pectin fruit requires different ratios of fruit to sugar than low pectin fruit, and low pectin fruit will often require the addition of acid, such as lemon juice, to help extract the pectin. Low pectin fruits will take longer to reach their setting point than high pectin fruit. Don't worry about all this because the recipes in this book have the quantities and ratios worked out for you. Not only do the recipes provide you with quantities suitable for making adequate amounts of jam, but also the ratio of fruit to other ingredients is given so that you can adjust the recipes to suit the quantity of fruit you have harvested.

Low pectin fruit include: apricots, blackberries, dessert cherries, and strawberries.
High pectin fruit include: apples, currants, damsons and green gooseberries.

Fruit
Although damaged fruit is fine to use, do discard any mouldy or overripe fruit. The riper it is the lower its pectin content and overripe fruit does not set well. It is not usually necessary to wash fruit, although you may wish to, particularly if it has been sprayed with chemicals. However, ensure that the fruit is dry when it is weighed so that the water does not affect the recipe. It is important to heat fruit

gently to remove as much pectin as possible from it. Always simmer the fruit until tender before adding the sugar because it will not soften further once the sugar is added.

Sugar

Granulated or caster sugar is the most commonly used sugar. You may see so called jam sugars in some shops. These have pectin added to them and really aren't necessary – ordinary sugar will do. Equally, preserving sugar is simply designed to dissolve well but isn't necessary if you follow the recipes correctly. It greatly helps the sugar to dissolve if it is warmed in the oven first. Once it is added to the fruit it is absolutely essential to make sure that all the sugar is dissolved before bringing it to the boil. Scrape your spoon along the sides and bottom of the pan checking for any grittiness that tells you it is still not fully dissolved. If you don't take the time and trouble to do this then the sugar will burn and stick to the bottom of your pan and your jam will be tainted.

Setting point

There are a number of ways to know when a jam has reached its setting point and it is usually worth doing more than one test to be sure. Firstly, if you have a jam thermometer then jam reaches its setting point at 104°C, 220 °F. Secondly, when you start the jam boiling, place a saucer in the freezer. When you think the jam is set, put a small teaspoon of jam on the saucer, wait for a moment for it to cool then push it with your fingernail. If the jam surfaces wrinkles then the jam is set. With experience you will also notice a definite change in the appearance of the bubbling jam once it has reached setting point. Once it has reached this point, remove it from the heat.

Warmed jars

Once you remove the sugar from the oven, put your jars in (without lids) to warm. There are a few reasons why you need warm jars to pour jam into. Firstly, pouring hot jam into cold jars could cause them to crack, secondly, once the lid is on and the jam cools down a very good seal is made, and thirdly, heating the jars kills any spores that might be lurking on them.

Transferring to jars

The easiest and safest way to transfer hot jam into hot jars is to use a ladle and a jam funnel. Jam funnels are like ordinary funnels with the bottom spout cut off to give a wider neck. They can be purchased from the same sort of places that supply preserving pans and are useful whenever you are transferring things into jars. Because the jam is hot, this is the most dangerous part of the process. Do not attempt to tip the jam from the pan into the jars. It is also worthwhile wearing appropriate shoes and an apron so as to avoid scolds from any minor spillages. Always handle the pan and the jars with oven gloves.

Jars
Although you can buy special jars for jams and preserves and can seal jars with waxed disks and plastic films, I feel this is unnecessary. Instead, I save jam and honey jars, and ask my friends and family to do the same (perhaps in return for filled jars once the jam is made!). It is important to wash them thoroughly, in a dishwasher if you have one or in very hot (boiling, even) water. They should also be thoroughly dry and dust free when you come to use them. Where the number of jars is indicated in a recipe, this is assuming the use of conventional 1 pound (454 g) jars. However, it is useful to have a variety of different sized jars saved because jam never comes out in exact quantities and the odd small jar will help you save every last drop of jam as well as provide a useful "sampler" jar.

Jelly making
Please read the jam making section as well because everything in there applies to jelly making too. However there are some extra points about jelly making as follows.

Jelly bags
If you intend to make a lot of jelly then it may well be worth investing in a jelly bag. These can be bought in the same places as other preserving equipment. At its most basic level, all a jelly bag comprises is a fine mesh with a mechanism for suspending it over a bowl overnight. On this principle, it is easy to improvise a jelly bag using a piece of muslin and some string. Before I was given a jelly bag, I used to use a large square of muslin in which I would put the pulped fruit. I then tied the square up in a bundle, tied a piece of string securely around its neck and suspended it from the handle of a kitchen cupboard over a bowl. Other people have used old tights as their mesh and have suspended it from the legs of an upturned stool.

The sieving technique
Whichever method you employ, always scold the mesh with boiling water first because this helps the liquid drain through. Because the jelly bag extracts only liquid from the fruit, it is unnecessary to puree the fruit first. It does, however, need to be mashed or pulped. It is also important to never be tempted to help the liquid through by squeezing it. The liquid that drips through is very pure and will give a

clear jelly. Squeezing the bag will result in a cloudy jelly. Once you have allowed the clear juices to drip through, it is worth squeezing the bag and using this liquid to make ice cream or fruit cheese (see recipes).

Transferring to jars
Use the jam making technique as your basic method for transferring jelly into jars with a couple of additional points. Firstly, tip the jar to one side as you pour in the jelly as this will help prevent air bubbles being trapped, which will spoil the appearance of your jelly. Secondly, do not move jelly whilst it is cooling down as this too can spoil the smooth appearance of your jelly.

Pickling
Pickling is a very straight forward preserving method that particularly suits some vegetables. The vegetables should be clean and in perfect condition. Often they can be preserved whole or may need to be sliced first. It is necessary to remove excess water from the vegetables before pickling and this can be done in one of two ways. They can be layered in a non-metallic bowl with salt and left for several hours or overnight. By morning the excess water should have come out of the vegetables which then need to be washed to remove the salt. Alternatively, they can be stored in very salty water (brine) for 24 hours before being thoroughly rinsed. The vegetables should also be dried well before pickling to prevent the vinegar becoming diluted. At this point most pickles can be jarred and covered in vinegar. Ordinary malt vinegar is perfectly fine, although some people might prefer the tang of pickling vinegar, which has been flavoured with spices. You may prefer to use malt vinegar and to add your own blend of spices. A ball of greaseproof paper should be placed in the neck of the jar to keep the vegetables submerged beneath the vinegar, particularly if the jar is not tightly packed with vegetables. The pickle should be left for about 2 months for the flavours to develop and then consumed within a year before the vegetables become soft.

Vegetables particularly suited for pickling are beetroot, cucumber, gherkin, onion and red cabbage.

Plastic containers for ice cream
The ideal containers for homemade ice cream are, of course, old ice cream containers. However, equally as suitable are the containers that Christmas puddings come in, or large yoghurt pots with re-sealable lids.

Pureeing

Several recipes require fruit to be pureed before being used. There are a number of ways to do this, requiring equipment of differing prices and sophistication. Usually the main aim of pureeing is to reduce the fruit to a liquid and to remove any seeds it contains. Therefore a way of squashing the fruit and then sieving it is required. One of the cheapest ways I found to do this is to buy a piece of muslin or cheesecloth, bundle the fruit into it and tie it up. Then, using your hands, squash the fruit and squeeze it through the cloth. This is very effective, although it is also messy and tiring on the hands and particularly unpleasant if the fruit are fresh from the fridge and cold! Another way is to place the fruit into a blender or food processor to liquidise then pour into a fine sieve (or sieve lined with muslin) and force the liquid through with a wooden spoon. I have recently purchased a "food strainer" (from Lakeland Ltd.) that winds the fruit through a corkscrew devise, squashing and sieving as it goes. This is very easy to use and effective but obviously quite specialised.

Steaming

Steaming equipment

Some people steam all their vegetables whilst others prefer boiling or even pressure-cooking. There are, however, some vegetables with delicate natures that do best when steamed. There are a whole variety of different steamers on the market from simple inserts to all-inclusive electrical appliances. At its most basic, steaming can be successfully done with an insert in a saucepan that lifts the vegetables above the water level.

Method

The handy thing about inserts is that they are also useful when blanching (see Freezing above). To use one of these, pour enough cold water into the bottom of the pan so that it just enters the steamer. Place a lid on the pan and heat. The water will boil and the vegetables will be cooked in the steam above. Steaming usually only takes a few minutes but this varies depending on the vegetable. Vegetables that are best steamed are broccoli, calabrese, mangetout, asparagus.

Stock

Uses

Stock is an essential ingredient of many recipes, particularly soups and casseroles. Throughout the recipes you will see both recipes for making stock and stock as an ingredient. Below are a few general pointers about the making, storage and types of stock. Although it is possible to simply use a stock cube, homemade stocks tend to be far superior and can be easily made either when required or as a convenient opportunity presents itself.

Meat stocks
Meat stocks are generally made when roasting a piece of meat. It is quite rare to find giblets these days inside chickens but other birds, such as duck or goose, do still come with their giblets. These can be boiled up in some water with suitable seasoning to produce a meat stock. If the meat came on the bone then the bone can be boiled once the meat has been removed, along with any remaining stuffing or a few addition herbs and onion. However, all roast meats run juices into the roasting dish when they cook and these too can be used as the basis of stock. It is best in this situation to remove the juices throughout the cooking process because if they are left in the dish until the end of the cooking time they will burn. You may, of course, use the juices immediately to make gravy but surplus gravy can be diluted to make a suitable stock. Another good source of meat stock is from a casserole. This usually requires a stock to begin with but during the cooking, a new stock develops which can be saved.

Fish stocks
Fish stock can be made by boiling up the pieces of fish that you would not wish to eat, such as the head, fins, skin and bones. Shellfish, such as prawns, can also be added to provide flavour, along with suitable herbs such as tarragon, parsley, bay and/or fennel. Vegetables such as carrot, leek or onion can also add flavour. You might also like to add a lemon or its juice and white wine.

Vegetable stocks
These are probably the easiest to make. You can make up a batch of vegetable stock specially using suitable vegetables such as leeks or onions, carrots, celery and potatoes, along with herbs, particularly bay and garlic, and seasoning. Alternatively, you can simply save the cooking water from a variety of vegetables when it comes to serving a meal, although the flavour is not as sophisticated. Simple vegetable stocks can be made with individual vegetables such as onion or leek by boiling up that vegetable and saving the cooking water.

Storing stocks
There are two main ways to store a stock for later use. One is to pour the hot liquid into a warmed jar with a "safety button" and seal it immediately. As it cools the button should become depressed and the stock will keep for several months. Alternatively, poor the stock into a

suitable container, allow it to cool then freeze it. Both methods allow any fat in the stock (from meat stocks) to float to the surface and become solid. This helps to form a seal, which keeps the stock preserved, but can be removed before reheating to avoid excessive fat in the recipe. It is useful to have a supply of stocks available because it is much more convenient not to have the additional burden of preparing a stock when following a recipe.

How much to grow

Amount:
This is a rough guide to how much you might want to grow to be self-sufficient in a particular crop (depending on how much you like it!). Clearly, you are unlikely to have space for everything so you might want to reduce the numbers. However, remember that you will not have all these crops growing at the same time. This is typically what I would grow in any year on two allotment plots and in two very small gardens. The number of rows assumes a 5 foot (1.2 m) row.

Interesting varieties to try:
These are some of the more unusual varieties of particular plants that you might want to look out for to add a bit of novelty.

Annual or perennial:
This is a suggestion of how you should grow the plant rather than whether something is strictly an annual or perennial. For example, some of these crops are perennial in warmer climes but only grow as an annual outside here. Others, such as carrot and celery, are biennial but are best grown as an annual.

Stored or fresh seed:
Most seeds successfully germinate even if they have been kept for a year or more. However, some will fail to germinate or have a very poor rate if older seeds are used so fresh seed is recommended. No suggestion here indicates that it should be bought as a plant.

Plant	Amount	Interesting varieties to try	Annual or perennial	Stored or fresh seed
Apple	1 tree	Mini	P	
Asparagus	12 crowns		P	
Aubergines	2-6 plants	Mini	A (P in heated greenhouse)	S
Basil	2-4 rows	Purple, lemon	A	S
Bay	1 plant		P	S
Beetroot	4-6 rows	Golden or pink and white stripes	A	S
Broad beans	8-10 rows	Crimson flowered	A	S
Broccoli	10-20 plants	White	A	S
Calabrese	10-20 plants	Mini	A	S

Cape gooseberries	10-20 plants		A (or P in heated greenhouse)	S
Carrots	4-6 rows	Round	A	S
Celery	2-3 rows	Pink	A	S
Cherry	1 tree		P	
Chives	2 plants		P	S
Climbing beans	20-60 plants		A	S
Courgettes	2-4 plants	Round	A	S
Cucumber	2-6 plants	Round	A	S
Currants	1-3 plants		P	
Dwarf beans	2-4 rows		A	S
Fennel	1 plant	Bronze	P	
Florence fennel	2-4 rows		A	S
Garlic	2-4 × bulbs		A	F
Gherkins	1-2 plants		A	S
Grape	1 vine		P	
Japanese onions	2 rows		A	S
Kale	10-20 plants	Purple	A	S
Leeks	20-60 plants		A	S
Lettuce	2-4 rows		A	S
Mangetout	2-4 rows		A	S
Marjoram	1 plant	Golden	A or P	S
Melons	2-6 plants		A	S
Mint	1 plant	Numerous	P	S
Onions	1-3 × 250 g	Red	A	F
Oregano	1 plant	Golden	A or P	S
Oriental leaves	2-4 rows		A	S
Parsnips	2-4 rows		A	F
Peach	1 tree	Mini	P	
Pear	1 tree	Mini	P	
Peas	5-8 rows	Purple flowered and/or purple podded	A	S
Peppers	2-6 plants	Numerous	A (P in heated greenhouse)	S
Plum	1 tree		P	
Potatoes	10-80 tubers		A	F

Pumpkins	1-2 plants		A	S
Raspberries	6-15 canes		P	
Red cabbage	5 plants		A	S
Rocket	1-2 rows		A	S
Rosemary	1-2 plants		P	S
Sage	1-2 plants	Purple	P	S
Savory	1 plant		P	S
Shallots	2-4 × 500 g		A	F
Spinach	1-2 rows		A	S
Spring onions	2-4 rows		A	S
Strawberries	10 plants		P	
Sweetcorn	12 – 70 plants		A	F
Tarragon	1 plant		P	
Thyme	3-6 plants	Lemon	P	S
Tomatoes	10-40 plants	Pink, purple, green, yellow or stripy fruit	A	S
Turnips	2-4 rows		A	S
Watercress	1 container		A	S
Winter spring onions	2 rows		A	S

Useful Webpages

Photographs

You will have noticed that this book does not contain pictures. If you wish to view photographs, pleased visit

http://community.webshots.com/user/hazelrockbox.

This is an ongoing project and more photos will be added with time so it will be worth returning every now and then.

Seeds, plants and sundries

Useful products can be bought at Hazel's Homegrown Ebay store at http://stores.ebay.co.uk/Hazels-Homegrown. These include seeds, seedlings, and a selection of other useful seasonal products. Hazel can also be contacted via the Ebay store using email to either ask a question about a product or for any other question relating to the growing or eating of your own food.

Other help

As well as contacting Hazel directly via the Ebay store, you may also like to join the kitchen garden discussion group at:

http://groups.yahoo.com/group/kitchengardens.

This has about 550 members at the time of writing who ask and answer numerous questions everyday.

Recipe Index by ingredient

	Sausage hotpot	October	173
	Winter salad	December	196
Blackcurrants	Blackcurrant and raisin flapjacks	July	90
	Blackcurrant cheesecake	July	90
	Blackcurrant crumble	July	90
	Blackcurrant ice cream	July	90
	Blackcurrant jam	July	90
	Blackcurrant jelly	July	90
	Blackcurrant muffins	July	90
	Summer fruits in cassis	July	90
Broad beans	Broad bean and savory soup	August	117
	Broad beans with bacon	June	68
Broccoli	Broccoli and garlic dressing	March	38
	Broccoli and salmon quiche	March	38
	Broccoli and salmon risotto	March	38
Calabrese	Piccalilli	September	153
	Smoked salmon and calabrese quiche	December	196
Carrot	Bolted vegetable stock	May	58
	Borscht (beetroot soup)	August	117
	Chicken and leek casserole	February	31
	Chicken and vegetable pie	October	173
	Fish pie	January	7
	Guinea fowl with carrot, courgette and port	September	153
	Mixed salad	August	117
	Sausage hotpot	October	173
	Steak and tomato pie	August	117
	Sweet and sour chicken and rice	September	153
	Vegetable stock	October	173
	Winter salad	December	196
	Chicken and potato bake	July	90
Celery	Bolted vegetable stock	May	58
	Celery Soup	April	48
	Cucumber chutney	August	117
	Mixed salad	August	117
	Vegetable stock	October	173
Celery leaves	Pea and bacon soup	July	90
Cherry	Cherry and ginger sauce	June	68
	Cherry and redcurrant jam	June	68
	Cherry pie	June	68
Chives	Duck with herbs and red fruit jelly	July	90
	Garlic chive butter (variations)	September	153
	Gherkin and mayonnaise dip	July	90
	Mixed salad	August	117

	Tomato sauce for pasta	August	117
	Vegetable stock	October	173
Garlic chives	Garlic chive butter	September	153
	Mixed salad	August	117
	Winter salad	December	196
Gherkins	Gherkin and mayonnaise dip	July	90
	Gherkin Tzatziki	July	90
	Pickled gherkins	July	90
Gooseberry	Gooseberry chutney	June	68
	Gooseberry jelly	July	90
	Strawberry and gooseberry jam	June	68
Haricot beans	Homemade baked beans	October	173
Japanese onions	Duck in oyster sauce with spring and Japanese onions	May	58
Leek	Bolted vegetable stock	May	58
	Chicken and leek casserole	February	31
	Chicken and vegetable pie	October	173
	Leek and cheese mashed potato	January	7
	Leek stock	February	31
	Sausage hotpot	October	173
Lemon balm	Fish seasoning	September	117
Lemon thyme	Broccoli and salmon quiche	March	38
	Fish seasoning	September	153
Lettuce	Broad beans with bacon	June	68
	Mixed salad	August	117
Mangetout	Stir-fried chicken with mangetout and spring onions	June	68
Marjoram	Pasta and pizza herb mix	September	153
Marrow	Piccalilli	September	153
Melon	Melon and cherry sticks	December	196
Mint	Guinea fowl with carrot, courgette and port	September	153
Onion	Asparagus stem soup	May	58
	Aubergine, courgette and tomato bake	August	117
	Beetroot and apple chutney	September	153
	Borscht (beetroot soup)	August	117
	Braised spiced red cabbage	December	196
	Broad bean and savory soup	August	117
	Broad beans with bacon	June	68
	Broccoli and salmon risotto	March	38
	Celery Soup	April	48
	Cheese and onion tarts	December	196
	Chicken and vegetable pie	October	173

	Christmas stuffing	December	196
	Courgettes with oregano	June	68
	Cucumber chutney	August	117
	Gooseberry chutney	June	68
	Homemade baked beans	October	173
	Home-made pizzas	November	185
	Pea and bacon soup	July	90
	Piccalilli	September	153
	Pork chops with sage mustard	May	58
	Spinach and lemon soup	April	38
	Steak and tomato pie	August	117
	Tomato and basil ketchup	August	117
	Vegetable stock	October	173
	Watercress soup	May	58
Oregano	Courgettes with oregano	June	68
	Pasta and pizza herb mix	September	153
Oriental leaves	Winter salad	December	196
Parsley	Celery Soup	April	48
	Garlic chive butter (variations)	September	153
Parsnips	Mashed parsnips	December	196
Peas	Chicken and vegetable pie	October	173
	Pea and bacon soup	July	90
	Sweet and sour chicken and rice	September	153
Peppers	Home-made pizzas	November	185
Plum	Plum jam	August	117
	Plum and mulled wine jam	August	117
	Plum and orange mincemeat	August	117
Potato	Beetroot and cucumber potato salad	August	117
	Borscht (beetroot soup)	August	117
	Chicken and leek casserole	February	31
	Chicken and potato bake	July	90
	Fish pie	January	7
	Mashed potatoes with cheese	January	7
	Pea and bacon soup	July	90
	Potato wedges	December	196
	Roast potatoes	December	196
	Sausage hotpot	October	173
	Watercress soup	May	58
Raspberries	Duck with herbs and red fruit jelly	July	90
	Raspberry and port jelly	July	90
	Raspberry chewies	July	90
	Raspberry ice cream	July	90
	Raspberry jam	July	90

	Redcurrant, raspberry and sherry jelly	July	90
	Summer fruits in cassis	July	90
Red cabbage	Braised spiced red cabbage	December	196
	Pickled cabbage	September	153
	Red cabbage and ginger	November	185
	Sweet and sour chicken and rice	September	153
Redcurrants	Duck with herbs and red fruit jelly	July	90
	Redcurrant, raspberry and sherry jelly	July	90
	Summer fruits in cassis	July	90
	Cherry and redcurrant jam	June	68
Rocket	Mixed salad	August	117
	Winter salad	December	196
Rosemary	Apple and rosemary jelly	August	117
	Bolted vegetable stock	May	58
	Chicken and leek casserole	February	31
	Chicken and potato bake	July	90
	Christmas stuffing	December	196
	Duck with herbs and red fruit jelly	July	90
	Fish seasoning	September	153
	Herb mustard	May	58
	Red tomato chutney	August	117
	Roast beef with rosemary mustard	May	58
	Sausage hotpot	October	173
	Steak and tomato pie	August	117
	Vegetable stock	October	173
Sage	Apple and sage cheese	August	117
	Bolted vegetable stock	May	58
	Chicken and leek casserole	February	31
	Chicken and potato bake	July	90
	Chicken and vegetable pie	October	173
	Christmas stuffing	December	196
	Duck with herbs and red fruit jelly	July	90
	Herb mustard	May	58
	Pork and apple burgers	August	117
	Pork chops with sage mustard	May	58
	Red tomato chutney	August	117
	Sage seasoning	September	153
	Sausage hotpot	October	173
	Vegetable stock	October	173
Savory	Broad bean and savory soup	August	117
Shallot	Asparagus stem soup	May	58
	Chicken casserole with shallots and courgettes	September	153
	Christmas stuffing	December	196

	Guinea fowl with carrot, courgette and port	September	153
	Pasta and pizza herb mix	September	153
	Piccalilli	September	153
	Pickled onions	August	117
	Pork chops with sage mustard	May	58
	Red tomato chutney	August	117
	Sage seasoning	September	153
	Tasty chicken drumsticks	December	196
	Tomato sauce for pasta	August	117
Spinach	Spinach and lemon soup	April	48
Spring onion	Winter salad	December	196
	Chicken and potato bake	July	90
	Duck in oyster sauce with spring and Japanese onions	May	58
	Mixed salad	August	117
	Stir-fried chicken with mangetout and spring onions	June	68
Strawberries	Strawberry cheesecake	December	196
	Posh preserved strawberry dessert	June	68
	Strawberry and cherry flapjacks	June	68
	Strawberry and gooseberry jam	June	68
	Strawberry and marshmallow ice cream	June	68
	Strawberry and orange conserve	June	68
	Strawberry crumble muffins	June	68
	Strawberry ice cream	June	68
	Strawberry Jam	June	68
	Summer fruits in cassis	July	90
Sweetcorn	Chicken and vegetable pie	October	153
	Home-made pizzas	November	185
	Sweet and sour chicken and rice	September	153
Tarragon	Broccoli and salmon quiche	March	38
	Fish seasoning	September	153
Thyme	Borscht (beetroot soup)	August	117
	Celery Soup	April	48
	Chicken and leek casserole	February	31
	Chicken and potato bake	July	90
	Duck with herbs and red fruit jelly	July	90
	Herb mustard	May	58
	Pasta and pizza herb mix	September	153
	Red tomato chutney	August	117
	Sausage hotpot	October	173
	Vegetable stock	October	173

Cooking tips

Printed in the United Kingdom
by Lightning Source UK Ltd.
103001UKS00001B/63